MOSES

MOSES

THE SERVANT OF GOD

F. B. Meyer

CHRISTIAN LITERATURE CRUSADE
Fort Washington, Pennsylvania 19034

CHRISTIAN LITERATURE CRUSADE

U.S.A.
Box 1449, Fort Washington, PA 19034

First American Edition 1978
under special arrangement with
Marshall, Morgan & Scott, Ltd.

ISBN 0-87508-354-4

PREFACE

THE conception of Moses, which I have elaborated in the following chapters, was suggested years ago by contrast with Michael Angelo's statue of him, colossal in proportions, hewn in stone.

Yet one turns away from that mighty head, that pregnant brow, that towering height, hopeless of repeating aught of a life, which, if that conception be the true one, must have had so little in common with our own. It is a comfort, therefore, to turn to the record of the New Testament, which tells that he did not spring at a leap to the throne on which he has sat through the ages, but that his character took years to form, and that his mighty deeds were due, not to some rare combination of personal qualities, but to the faith which he had in common with the rank and file of the great army of the saints.

I have tried, therefore, to show that Moses was a man like other men; with great qualities that needed to be developed and improved; with flaws that veined the pure marble of his character; with deficiencies that had rendered him powerless but for the all-sufficient grace that he learned to appropriate; and that he wrought his life-work by the simplicity of his faith, by communion with God, and by becoming a channel through which the Divine purpose was achieved.

F. B. MEYER

CONTENTS

I

OUR STANDPOINT

"By faith, Moses. . . ."
—HEB. xi. 24.

THE WRITER of the Epistle to the Hebrews lays bare the secret of the marvels effected by the heroes of Hebrew story. Obedient to his summons, they range themselves in one great battalion, and with united breath, cry, Why marvel ye at these things? or why look ye so earnestly on us, as though by our own power or holiness we had effected them? The God of Abraham, of Isaac, and of Jacob, the God of our fathers, made bare his holy arm and wrought by us. And his name, through faith in his name, hath done all these wonderful works.

We make a profound mistake in attributing to these men extra-ordinary qualities of courage, and strength of body or soul. To do so is to miss the whole point of the reiterated teaching of Scripture. They were not different from ordinary men, except in their faith. In many respects it is most likely that they were inferior to ourselves. We should probably be much surprised if we were to encounter them in the daily walks of modern life, and should find it almost impossible to believe that they wrought such prodigies of valour, endurance, and deliverance. Gideon and Barak, Samson and Jephthah, were rather of the type of the sturdy Borderers of olden days, whose wild doings kept our northern counties in constant agitation, than like our modern clerics or Christian philanthropists. But there was one characteristic common to them all, which lifted them above ordinary men, and secured for them a niche in the Temple of Scripture—that they had a marvellous faculty of faith; which, indeed, is but the capacity of the human heart for God. Four times over this is cited as the secret of all that Moses did for his people.

The same truth is repeatedly corroborated in the teaching of our Lord. He never stops to ask what may be the specific quantity of

9

power, or wisdom, or enthusiasm, which exists in his disciples. In his judgment these things are as the small dust of the balance, not to be taken into serious consideration, and not likely to affect the aggregate results of a man's life. But his incessant demand is for *faith*. If only there be faith, though it be but as a grain of mustard-seed, sycamore trees can be uprooted; mountains cast into the midst of the sea; and demons exorcised from their victims. To a father He once said: "There is no *if* in my power; it is in thy faith. If thou canst believe, all things are possible to him that believeth."

And what is this faith? It is not some inherent power or quality in certain men, by virtue of which they are able to accomplish special results unrealized by others. It is rather the power of putting self aside that God may work unhindered through the nature. It is the attitude of heart which, having ascertained the will of God, and being desirous of becoming an organ for it, goes on to expect that God will work out his purposes through its medium. It is, in brief, that capacity for God which appropriates Him to its uttermost limit, and becomes the channel or vehicle through which He passes forth to bless mankind. The believer is the God-filled, the God-moved, the God-possessed man; and the work which he effects in the world is not his, but God's through him.

There are, therefore, these necessary conditions of all true faith:

The sense of helplessness and nothingness.
An absolute assurance of being on God's plan.
Entire consecration, that He may work out his will through heart and life.
The daily food of promise.
A daring to act, in utter independence of feeling, on a faith which reckons absolutely on the faithfulness of God.

It will be our contention throughout our study of the remarkable life before us, that, though Moses may have had commanding features of mind and body, and have been versed in all the learning of his time; yet the marvellous outcome of his life-work was not due to any of these qualities, but to the faith which knit his soul to God. His faith sufficed to do what all his other qualities, without his faith, must have failed in doing.

We hope to go further, and show that all the blessings which God in his mindfulness of his covenant bestowed on Israel, came to that rebellious and stiff-necked people through the channel of Moses' faith. It is God's method to seek the co-operation of man in the execution of his purposes, and to fulfil his promise through his servants' faith. In this case it was Moses who was called into partnership with Jehovah, and it was through his faith that God fulfilled the promise made to Abraham, Isaac, and Jacob.

Each of the above-mentioned conditions of a mighty faith was fulfilled in the history of Moses.

He was allowed to make his first efforts for the emancipation of his people in the energy of his own strength, and to fail egregiously; so that he fled away to Midian, abandoning all hope of delivering them, and spending his years in solitude and exile, until it was with the greatest difficulty that he could be induced to undertake the Divine commission. He was reduced to the last extreme of helpless nothingness when the burning bush flamed in his path, a symbol of utter weakness, possessed and indwelt yet unconsumed by God, who is a consuming fire.

He could have no doubt as to God's plan; for that lay unfolded before him in the promise made to Abraham long years before, fixing four hundred years as the limit of the Egyptian sojourn. And, in addition, God distinctly told him that He had come down to deliver.

He was as thoroughly yielded to the purpose of God, as the staff which he held in his hand was to his own will. Hence his chosen name, "the servant of the Lord"; and the constant recurrence of the phrase, "as the Lord commanded Moses."

He fed daily on the promises of God, pleading them in prayer, and leaning his whole weight upon them. And he often knew what it was to leave behind him the familiar and tried, for the strange and new; at the bidding of God, he stepped out, though there seemed nothing to tread upon, launching himself and three millions of people absolutely on the care of God, assured that God's faithfulness could not fail.

His faith made Moses all he was. We shall see this more clearly as we proceed. For it is our eager desire to learn exactly how such a faith as his was produced. Why should we not have it? God's methods are never out of date. It is certain that we shall have his faith, if we but pay the price of enduring his discipline. And if only we possessed his faith, why should we not see another Exodus?— seas seamed with paths of salvation; foes defied; chains snapped;

captives emancipated; and Jehovah worshipped with songs of triumph ! Surely there is no limit to the possibilities of a life which has become the aperture or channel through which God can pour Himself forth.

Are you willing to die to your own strength; to forsake your own plans for God's; to seek out and do his will absolutely; to take up the attitude of entire and absolute surrender to his purposes; to feed daily on the promises of God, as a girl on the pledge of her absent lover; to step out in faith, reckoning, without emotion of any kind, on the faithfulness of God, only fully persuaded that He will perform all that He has promised ? Then surely through you God will, here or hereafter, work as in the times of old, of which our fathers have told us.

It is certain, as the present age draws to a close, that God has great schemes on hand which must shortly be realized. According to his invariable method He will have to perform them through the instrumentality and faith of men; the one question is, Are we in such a condition, is our faith of such a nature, that He can work by us to the glory of his holy Name ? Let us ponder well the lessons taught in the life and character of Moses, that in due time we too may become vessels meet for the Master's use, and prepared to every good work.

II

His Mother's Faith

"By faith Moses, when he was born, was hid three months of his parents, because they saw he was a proper child; and they were not afraid of the king's commandment."
—HEB. xi. 23.

IT WAS on a very unfriendly world that the little babe opened his eyes. Without, all was as fair as nature and art could make it. Hard by the mean cottage, which for a brief space was to shelter him, the mighty Nile rolled between its reedy banks, reflecting on its broad bosom the deep azure of the arching heavens by day, and the starry constellations of the night. Within the easy distance of a maiden's morning walk stood the great city of Memphis, metropolis of Egypt and seat of the Court; centre of trade, and art, and war, and religion; the focus to which the national life converged.

Past that cottage-home would go royal processions, as in solemn state the monarch went forth to war, or came down to the Nile brink to worship. Priests from all parts of the land would pass it on their way to the mighty Temple of Phthah, whose pillared avenues, and sculptured galleries, and hieroglyphed chambers, were the result of centuries of industry, and told the story of the generations that had built them; but how little would they dream that the site of that humble cottage would attract the interest of generations to the end of time, when their lordly temple had fallen into an indistinguishable heap! And the perpetual supply of leeks and melons and garlic, of barley and wheat and rye, of delicate fabrics from the loom, for which the Egyptians became so famous, of spice and balm for the vast City of the Dead, and of all the multitudinous provision for the demands of a large and wealthy population, must have covered the neighbouring roads with an unceasing stream of camels and asses and caravans, and the river with an innumerable flotilla of boats, barges, and ships. Not far away, across the level sands, were the

Pyramids, which even then were becoming venerable with age, and were destined to remain for forty centuries, witnesses alike to man's instinctive belief in his immortality, and to his selfish indifference to the anguish of his fellows. Amid these circumstances of wealth and splendour the little babe was born to an unkindly lot.

He belonged to an alien race.—More than three hundred years before, the forefathers of his people had emigrated from the neighbouring land of Palestine, at the invitation of the Prime Minister of the time, who was connected with them by the ties of kinship and race. The king had welcomed them as likely to be valuable allies; for he also belonged to a foreign race, and sat on an unstable throne. At his command they had settled in the best of the land, a strip of green, called Goshen, situated amid vast tracks of sand. There they prospered and multiplied, till they numbered near upon two million souls. But they remained as distinct a people as they are now in every nation under heaven, and as such were open to suspicious hate.

He belonged to an oppressed race.—A different dynasty had succeeded to that which welcomed them, and one to whom the name of Joseph had no charm. At the time of which we write a tiny cloud of impending war trembled on the Eastern sky, and suggested to the reigning monarch the fear that there might be a coalition between his enemies and the Hebrew race, which had grown into such numbers and might, as to be very formidable. He resolved, therefore, to wear them out, and to reduce both their numbers and their spirit by the rigour of their lot.

Suddenly, the shepherds of Goshen found themselves drafted for service in the brickfields, under the eye and whip of cruel taskmasters, who exacted from them daily a certain tale of bricks; or they performed service in the field, drawing water from the river for the irrigation of the land, and toiling in the cultivation of the soil. "And all their service wherein they made them serve was with rigour"; as if every occasion was eagerly taken advantage of for dealing out cruel and merciless punishment.

The father of the little household was, probably, compelled to bear his share in the bondage and blows which made the existence of his people so bitter. From morning to night he would toil, naked, beneath the burning sun, returning often with bleeding wounds torn open by the scourge, and inclined to question the very existence of God and his character for mercy. Very dark was the night which lay heavily on the chosen people in these years of cruel enslavement.

He was born at a time of unusual trouble.—The household consisted of father and mother, of an elder sister, some fifteen years of
age, marvellously gifted with the power of song, and of a little
brother, Aaron, a bright and merry boy of three years of age. When
the latter was born, there was apparently no special need of secrecy;
for the king was trying to attain his object by the vigorous policy
we have above described. But during the interval, he had discovered
that it was not stringent enough to attain his end; and he had, therefore, added to it a scheme for the destruction of all the male children,
by casting them into the river as they were born.

It is not likely that this decree was in active operation for more
than a few months. It was a spasm of cruelty which was inspired
by sudden fear; but was too utterly opposed to the better instincts
of human nature to secure for itself a permanent position in the
practice of Pharaoh's subordinates. But whilst it lasted, it was the
bitterest element in all that bitter sorrow. Privation, hardship, scorn,
and rigour, are easy to bear, if only the beloved circle of the home is
left intact; but when that is threatened, and the little fledglings are
menaced by the bird of prey, the waters of a full cup are wrung out.

Generally, the birth of a child, and especially of a boy, was
heralded with unstinted joy: but now it was the subject of anxiety,
and almost of dread. There was no glad anticipation, no welcome,
no rapture, to compensate for the mother's anguish, in the thought
that a man was born into the world. Yet in spite of all, "the people
multiplied and became very mighty." The edict remained in operation for but a short time, but it was during its enforcement that
Moses was born. This is God's way. In the darkest hours of the
night his tread draws near across the billows. As the day of execution is breaking, the angel comes to Peter's cell. When the scaffold
for Mordecai is complete, the royal sleeplessness leads to a reaction
in favour of the threatened race. Ah, soul, it may have to come to
the worst with thee ere thou art delivered; but thou wilt be ! God
may keep thee waiting; but He will ever be mindful of his covenant,
and will appear to fulfil his inviolable word.

But he was the child of believing parents.—We know but little of
them. The father is said to have been "a man of the house of Levi,"
and we learn afterwards that his name was Amram, and descended
from Kohath, the son of Levi; but the tribe of Levi had then no
special importance—in fact, it seemed destined to be divided in
Jacob, and scattered in Israel. The mother, Jochebed, belonged to

the same tribe, and, indeed, was related to her husband in a closer consanguinity than was afterwards permitted. They were humble folk, glad enough to receive "wages" from the hand of wealth and royalty; but they preserved the best religious traditions of their nation, and in this contrasted favourably with many of their race.

Dean Stanley has shown that the sojourn in Egypt had produced a very deleterious result on the children of Israel. "The old freedom, the old energy, above all, the old religion of the patriarchal age, had faded away." There are clear evidences in the later Scriptures that the people participated in the idolatrous rites of the land of their adoption. "Your fathers," said Joshua, "served other gods in Egypt" (Josh. xxiv. 14). And through the lips of Ezekiel, Jehovah reminded the nation, at a later date, of their early unfaithfulness. "In the day that I lifted up mine hand unto them, to bring them forth of the land of Egypt into a land flowing with milk and honey, the glory of all lands. Then said I unto them, Cast ye away every man the abominations of his eyes, and defile not yourselves with the idols of Egypt; I am the Lord your God. But they rebelled against Me, and would not hearken unto Me; they did not every man cast away the abominations of their eyes, neither did they forsake the idols of Egypt" (Ezek. xx. 6–8). The Sabbath was forgotten; the rite of circumcision, the significant token of the covenant, fell into disuse; the comparative purity of their forefathers proved unable to resist the licentious attractions of heathen festivals, to which in after years they perpetually recurred.

But evidently there were some families who remained faithful amid the prevalent corruption. Amongst these was that into which this child was born. The sacred covenant between God and their race was reverently remembered, and held by a faith which dared to believe that, sooner or later, God must interpose. The treasured stories which are preserved to us in the book of Genesis would be carefully taught to the children as soon as their hearts could appreciate, and their memories preserve them. The first-born, Aaron, would be set apart, with some kind of consecration, to perform the functions of the priest of the household. And Miriam, the first Mary of Scripture, would be taught to use her sweet, clear, voice in the praise and worship of the God of their fathers.

But their religious life was still more manifested by their faith. "By faith Moses, when he was born, was hid three months of his parents, because they saw he was a proper child; and they were not afraid of the king's commandment." We have often been furnished with a picture depicting the anxiety with which his parents received their new-born babe, the distress of Amram, and the fears of Jochebed. Such a picture may be true of others of the Hebrew parents, but it is not true of them. "They were not afraid." When it was announced to Jochebed that she had borne a boy, she was enabled to cast the care of him on God, and to receive the assurance that he should come to no hurt. And as the couple bent over their child, in that peasant's hut, and saw his exceeding goodliness, the conviction grew in their hearts that a great destiny awaited him; and that in some way he would live to see the expiration of the time of slavery, foretold centuries before in words which had passed from lip to lip, the one rift of light amid the blackness of their night. Josephus says that a dream announced to Amram that Moses would be the deliverer of his people.

Could those down-trodden serfs ever forget what God had told their great ancestor, when the horror of a great darkness had fallen on his soul? "Know of a surety that thy seed shall be a stranger in a land that is not theirs, and shall serve them, and they shall afflict them four hundred years . . . but in the fourth generation they shall come hither again" (Gen. xv. 13, 16). The slow-moving years had at last accumulated to the prescribed number. Four hundred years had nearly, if not quite, elapsed. The promise must be on the point of fulfilment. The words, "they shall come out" (Gen. xv. 14) rang like a peal of bells in the mother's heart; and there was a confidence nurtured by the Spirit of God, and by the loveliness of her child, who was "goodly" (Exod. ii. 2), "proper" (Heb. xi. 23), and "exceeding fair" (Acts vii. 20), that in some way he should share in that Exodus.

She was not always on the *qui vive* for the step of officer or mid-wife. She would take all ordinary precaution; but she would never give way to excessive fear. Sometimes when her heart grew sick she would betake herself to her knees, and plead the Divine promise on which she had been caused to hope. The whole family lived on that woman's faith, as men live on bread; and God's angels bent over the unconscious babe, shielding it with their tenderest care, and whispering their love-words into its ear. Finally, the mother was led by the good Spirit of God to weave the papyrus rushes into a little ark, or boat, coating it with bitumen, to make it impervious to wet. There she put the child with many a kiss, closed the lid upon its sweet face, with her own hands bore it to the water's edge, and placed it tenderly among the flags that grew there. She knew that Pharaoh's daughter came there to bathe, and it might be that she would notice and befriend the little foundling. Or, if not, the God whom she trusted would help her in some other way. But all the while she never lost her simple, steadfast faith. "The Lord was her light and her salvation: whom should she fear? The Lord was the strength of her life: of whom should she be afraid? When her enemies and foes came upon her to eat up her flesh, they would stumble and fall. Though an host should encamp against her, yet should she not fear."

Miriam was set to watch, not with any thought of harm that would ensue, whether from unfriendly hand, or from beast of prey, but simply to see "what would be done to him"; and Jochebed went back to her house, fighting a mother's natural anxiety by a faith which had enclasped the very arm of the living God, who could not fail her, though the heavens should fall, or the pyramids be hurled into the broad bosom of the Nile. That is faith. Can we wonder at the faith of the man who was born of such a mother, and nurtured in such a home?

III

" Come to Years "

"By faith, Moses, when he was come to years, refused to be called the son of Pharaoh's daughter."
—Heb. xi. 24.

It ALL befell according to the mother's faith. The princess, accompanied by a train of maidens, came to the river bank to bathe. She saw the ark among the flags, and sent her maid to fetch it. In the midst of the little group the lid was carefully uplifted; and their eyes were charmed with the sight of the beautiful face, whilst their hearts were touched with the whimper of the babe, who missed its mother, and was frightened by its unwonted surroundings and the many strange faces.

Quickly the woman's heart guessed the secret. The neighhourhood of Hebrew huts, the features and complexion of the babe, the unlikelihood of a mother forgetting her suckling child, the sudden recollection of the stern edict which her father had lately promulgated, all pointed to the inevitable conclusion, "This is one of the Hebrews' children." The sudden interposition of Miriam, who had eagerly and breathlessly watched the whole scene, with her naïve suggestion of fetching a Hebrew nurse, solved the problem of what should be done with the foundling almost as soon as it could have suggested itself. Quickly the child's mother stood before the princess, and received the precious burden from her hands; and as she did so, was there not something in her almost convulsive movement which revealed to that quick eye the secret of the little plot? Whether it were so or not, the story does not tell. But with what an ecstasy of joy would that mother pour out her heart when the door was closed on the little group? The child's life was secure beneath the powerful protection of Pharaoh's own daughter, who had said, "Nurse it for me." And the wages which she had promised would do more than provide for all their need. God had done "exceedingly abundantly."

19

How long the boy stayed in that lowly home we do not know—perhaps till he was four or five years old: but long enough, in any case, to know something of the perils and hardships of his people's lot; to learn those sacred traditions of their past, which he was afterwards to weave with such majestic simplicity into the Book of Genesis; and to receive into his heart the love of the only God, which was to become the absorbing passion and pole-star of his career. Priests, philosophers, and scholars, might do their best afterwards; but these things had been built into the growing structure of his soul, never again to be disintegrated from its fabric. What an encouragement is suggested by this record to mothers—to make the very most of the early years during which children are confided to their charge. The circumstances must be exceptional indeed under which that charge can be entrusted to others.

At last the time arrived when Thermutis claimed for her own the child whom she had rescued. He had now grown so beautiful that, Josephus tells us, passers-by stood still to look at him, and labourers their left work to steal a glance. The mother's heart must have suffered bitterly as she let her boy go into the unknown world within the great palace-gate; and very lonely must the little household have felt when the last kisses had been exchanged, the last instruction given, and the last prayer offered. What a crowd of tender thoughts, curious speculations, and eager yearnings must have followed the little nurseling of the Hebrew home, as his mother took him and brought him unto Pharaoh's daughter, and he became her son ! But, amid all, faith rose pre-eminent, and believed that He who had delivered the child from the perils of the Nile, would keep him pure and sweet amid the evils and fascinations of the Court.

What a magnificent land must Egypt have been in those days of which Herodotus and the hieroglyphic records speak ! The atmosphere was rainless; the Nile brought from afar the rich alluvial soil, that bore corn enough to feed the world; the banks of the river were covered with cities, villages, stately temples, and all the evidences of an advanced civilization; whilst mighty pyramids and colossal figures towered to a hundred feet in height. Seven millions of people throve on this green riband of territory; and whilst the great mass of them were probably poor and ignorant, the upper classes, and especially the priests, were remarkable for their familiarity with much of which we boast ourselves to-day.

The cream of all this was poured into the cup of Moses. He was brought up in the palace, and treated as the grandson of Pharaoh. If he rode forth into the streets, it would be in a princely equipage, amid the cries of "Bow the knee." If he floated on the Nile, it would be in a golden barge, amid the strains of voluptuous music. If he wished for aught, the almost illimitable wealth of the treasures of Egypt was within his reach.

When old enough he was probably sent to be *educated in the college*, which had grown up around the Temple of the Sun, and has been called "the Oxford of Ancient Egypt." There he would learn to read and write the mysterious hieroglyph; there, too, he would be instructed in mathematics, astronomy, and chemistry, in all of which the Egyptians were adepts. There, also, he would acquire a taste for music; so that in after days he could sing glad and triumphant songs of victory, and compose odes which embalmed the history of God's dealings with his people. How wonderfully was God fitting him for his after-life! Stephen says: "Moses was learned in all the wisdom of the Egyptians" (Acts vii. 22). Much of it was undoubtedly the merest folly; but much of it, also, stood him in good stead when he became the founder of a new state.

But Moses was something more than a royal student, spending his years in cultured refinement and lettered ease. *He was a statesman and a soldier.* Stephen tells us that he was "mighty in words and in deeds": mighty in words—there is the statesman; mighty in deeds—there the soldier. Josephus says that whilst he was still in his early manhood the Ethiopians invaded Egypt, routed the army sent against them, and threatened Memphis. In the panic the oracles were consulted; and on their recommendation Moses was entrusted with the command of the royal troops. He immediately took the field, surprised and defeated the enemy, captured their principal city, "the swamp-engirdled city of Meroë," and returned to Egypt laden with the spoils of victory.

Thus year followed year till he was forty years of age. Already the foremost positions of the State were open to him; and it seemed as if the river of his life would continue in the same bed, undiverted, and only waxing ever broader and deeper in its flow.

But, beneath all, another thought was always present with him, and gradually dwarfed all others as it grew within his soul. He could not forget that his parents were slaves; that the bondmen who were groaning in the brickfields beneath the lash of the task-masters were his brethren. He never lost the thought of that God to whom his mother had taught him to pray: and in his gayest, most successful moments, when sipping the intoxicating cup of earthly success, he could not rid himself of the impression that his destiny did not lie amid such surroundings as those, but was in some way to be associated with the fulfilment of that promise which he had heard so often from his mother's lips.

Thoughts like these would often cast strange shadows over his face, which baffled those who knew him best. His foster-mother might attribute the strange tinge of melancholy to ill-health or some unrequited love. His friends and companions would rally him on his absent-mindedness. His suite would often discuss the subject of their master's depression, and wonder as to its cause. But the mystery remained locked in his heart till his vague impressions had become settled resolves; and he broke, as gently as he might, the news to his benefactress that he could no longer hold the position to which she had raised him, or be called her son, but must step back to the lowly lot which was his by birth.

The announcement would be, perhaps, met by bitter tears and hot indignation on the part of her to whom he owed so much; but neither the one nor the other made him swerve by a hair's-breadth from his purpose. And how great a sensation must have been caused throughout the Court as the news leaked out ! In how many circles it would be discussed, and what different interpretations would be placed on it ! Some would attribute it to mortification or jealousy; others to the presence in his veins of base slave-blood; others to some scheme of ultimate self-aggrandizement. All would commiserate the princess, whose kindness seemed so rudely requited. But no one guessed the strength or purity of his hidden purpose, born of God, and nurtured by His good Spirit.

I.—Notice the Noble Ingredients in this Great Resolve. (1) *It was made in the full maturity of his powers.* The impulsive ardour of youth will sometimes lead a young heart to say, "This people shall be my people, and their God my God." But there was nothing of that kind here. It was the deliberate resolve of a man who had seen much of life, who knew all that could be urged from every side, and who was come to years. With nothing to gain and all to lose, after thoughtful examination, he descended from the footsteps of the loftiest throne in the world.

(2) *It was made when the fortunes of the children of Israel were at their lowest ebb.* They were slaves, were suffering affliction, and were reproached. For a palace there would be a hut; for luxury, hard fare and coarse food; for respect and honour, hatred and contempt; for the treasures of Egypt, poverty and want; for the society of the learned and *élite*, association with the ignorant and depraved. But none of these things moved him. He counted them as the small dust of the balance. With deliberate resolution he bowed his head beneath the yoke, albeit it was rough and heavy.

(3) *It was made when the pleasures of sin seemed most fascinating.* There is nothing gained in saying that there are no pleasures in sin. There are. The forbidden fruit is pleasant to the eye and luscious to the taste; the first steps along the broad road are over a carpet of velvet grass, enamelled with countless flowers; there are notes of dulcet sweetness in the syren's song, which ravish the heart. Temptation would have no power at all if it were not so. The keen thrill of pleasure is the bait, beneath which the great enemy of souls hides the inevitable hook. And Moses was not oblivious to all this; yet, in the heyday of his strength, in the prime of his manhood, in a court where continence and purity must have been unknown, he dared to forego it all.

(4) *It was made decisively.* Many would have tried to retain the proud position and to benefit their enslaved brethren at the same time; to temporize between an outward recognition of Osiris, and a heart-loyalty to Jehovah; to keep on good terms with court and brick-kiln. But there was no trace of this in the great renunciation which cut Moses off from the least association with the fond and fascinating associations of early life.

Are there not times in all our lives when a similar step has to be taken by ourselves? We have to die to much that is pleasant and attractive, in order to rise to our true life. Buried, to bear fruit; maimed, to enter life; laying our Isaac on the altar, to become the leader of the faithful; turning aside from the gate of a sunlit garden, to take a darker, stonier, path; renouncing what others hold without rebuke, because of some high purpose which has forced its way into the soul; choosing Gethsemane and Calvary and the grave, in fellowship with the Man of Sorrows; being willing to renounce friends, wealth, reputation, and success, and to be flung like a shipwrecked sailor on some lone shore, because of some vision that beckons us. Those who have done any one of these can understand, as others cannot, the nobility and greatness of Moses' choice.

II. THE THOUGHT WHICH LED TO IT. "By faith Moses refused...." Faith rests on promise; to her the promise is equivalent to fulfilment; and if only she has the one, she dares to count on the other as already hers. It matters comparatively little that the thing promised is not given; it is sure and certain, because God has pledged his word for it, and in anticipation she enters on its enjoyment. She weighs the things that she can touch against those which are only as yet foretold, because in her judgment the latter are as real as the former. Thus it was with Moses.

He believed God's promise to Abraham, that after four hundred years of bondage his people would come out; and he knew that that period had nearly expired. He cherished a fervent belief in that promise made to the chosen people, that from their ranks the true Deliverer would arise—a shadowy belief in the coming Messiah, which, notwithstanding its vagueness, he dared not forfeit. He believed that there was a destiny waiting for the chosen people in the long future, which would throw into shadow all the pomp and splendour of the magnificent Pharaoh. He believed that there was a recompense of reward awaiting them beyond the bourne and limit of Egypt, more glorious than the dazzling splendour of its highest rewards and honours. He evidently believed, what he expected his brethren to believe, that God would deliver them by his hand. And it was this that determined him.

Had he simply acted on what he saw, he had never left Pharaoh's palace. But his faith told him of things hidden from his contemporaries; and these altered his course, and led him to act in a way which to them was perfectly incomprehensible.

He did not simply close his eyes to the claims of Egypt, and steel his nerves against the threats of Pharaoh, isolating himself with the exclusiveness of a cynic: that might have been dictated by a strong and wise policy. But he did what he did, because he saw by faith what eye had not seen, or ear heard, or the heart conceived; and these things—that wealth and that reward—being so much better than anything Egypt could offer, he cheerfully took the path of affliction, of self-denial and reproach, which led to them.

See, child of God, what is within thy reach, if only thou wilt dare to deny thyself and take up thy cross ! Send the spies into the Land of Promise. Climb the delectable mountains, and put the telescope to thine eyes. And as the far more exceeding and eternal weight of glory breaks on thy vision, thou wilt be prepared to count all things else, which had seemed gain, to be loss and dung, and not worthy to be mentioned in the comparison. Is the renunciation hard? Do not forget that Christ is suffering with you in it all. His steps lie along this road. It is "the reproach of Christ"—a little phase of His long suffering through the sufferings of his people. He knows every step of the way, because He has so often traversed it in the experience of his own. There is no solace to the agonized soul so sweet as the perpetual mention of his dear name, as if it were conscious that in all its afflictions He is afflicted, and that the Angel of his presence is going at its side.

And who can estimate the result? The water streams from the smitten rock; the flower springs from the dead seed; the crystal river flows from the moraine of the glacier; the bright gold emerges from the dark mine and the cleansing fires. An Exodus and the birth of a nation of freemen were the outcome of this great renunciation.

IV

Deliverance by Main Force

"And seeing one of his brethren suffer wrong, he defended him, and avenged him that was oppressed, and smote the Egyptian. For he supposed his brethren would have understood how that God by his hand would deliver them: but they understood not."

—Acts vii. 24, 25.

There was true heroism in the act, when Moses stepped down from Pharaoh's throne to share the lot of his brethren. He might have contented himself by sending them money from the treasures of Egypt; but it was a greater and nobler thing to give himself. And the true religious instinct of his soul gleamed out as he did so. There was a revelation of the faith which had been kindled within him when he knelt at his mother's side in the slave-hut, and had survived all the adverse influences of the Egyptian Court, like a spark of fire living in the heart of black coals.

At the same time there was a great deal for him to learn. In after days he was to know the ways of the Lord—God would make them known to him (Psa. ciii. 7); but just now he was full of his own ways. In after days he was to be a hand, nerved, and used, and empowered by God Himself (Psa. lxxvii. 20); but now he was acting in his own self-energy—rash, impetuous, headstrong, girding himself and walking whither he would. In after days he was to be the meekest and least obtrusive of men, conscious to a fault of his own weakness, and at every step looking up for guidance and help; but now he leaned wholly on his own understanding, and, without taking counsel of God, thought to secure the emancipation of his people by the assertion of his will, and the forth-putting of his might.

Ah! there was the making of a saint in him; but it would take many a long year of lonely waiting and trial before this strong and self-reliant nature could be broken down, shaped into a vessel meet for the Master's use, and prepared for every good work. God's work can only be done by his chosen instruments, and they must be specially fitted for the service they are to render. That special adaptation is not natural to any of us, and can only come after years of deep and searching discipline.

I. THE FIRST ATTEMPT AT DELIVERANCE.—(1) *It sprang largely from human sympathy.* As soon as he reached Goshen his first act was to go out and see his brethren in the midst of their toils, working amid the conditions of the severest hardship. Brick-making in stiff clay-pits must always be arduous employment; but how much more so when an Egyptian sun shone vertically above them, and a task-master stood by with his heavy whip to punish the least attempt to flinch from toil or shirk the collar ! Imagine the accomplished courtier, the child of luxury and fashion, the man of letters and of mighty deeds, as he moves amid these long lines of slaves. At first it must have seemed very strange to him to realize that he was bound in bonds of such close kinship to these toiling, suffering, dying, Hebrews. " He went out unto his brethren." But this feeling must soon have given place to an intense commiseration, as he heard the nation sighing by reason of its bondage; and groaning under its accumulated sorrows, his soul would be filled with tender pity. But within a little, that pity for his people turned to indignation against their oppressors. Before he had taken many steps he came on one of the task-masters cruelly beating a Hebrew; and as he witnessed the horrid spectacle, the heavy blows falling on the unresisting quivering body, he could restrain himself no longer, and felled the caitiff lifeless to the ground, then bore away his body and buried it in the nearest sands, ever waiting to encroach on the more cultivated lands of Egypt.

It was a chivalrous act, well meant, and at least significant of the strength of the emotions pent up within him; but, after all, the mere impulse of pity would never have been strong enough to bear him through the weary years of the desert march. Beneath the repeated provocations of the people it must have given way. He could never have carried them as a nursing-father, or asked that he might be blotted out of the book of life for them, or pleaded with them for God. Nothing short of a reception of the Divine patience, let into his soul as the ocean waves find an inlet into some deeply-indented coast, could suffice for the demands which would be made on him in those coming terrible years.

Is there not a lesson here for many of God's workers ? They have not learned to distinguish between passion and principle, between impulse and a settled purpose. If some touching tale is told, some piteous appeal made for help, or some crowded gathering swept by a wave of missionary enthusiasm, they are the first to yield to the impulse, to volunteer their service, to give their money, and fling themselves into the breach. But, after all, this is not the loftiest motive for Christian service, and it certainly is not the most permanent. After a little while it dies down, and leaves us stranded as by a receding tide. It is better far to sacrifice the mere natural impulse for the strong sense of what is right, and what God requires. If we undertake a definite work because He calls us to it, because it is put before us as a duty for his sake, or because we are channels through which the unebbing torrent of his Divine pity is flowing, we have secured a principle of action which will bear us through disappointment, failure, and ingratitude. The way in which men treat us will make no difference to us, because all is done for Him.

(2) *It was premature.* God's time for the deliverance of his people was not due for forty years. The iniquity of the Amorites had not reached its full, though it was nearing the brim of the cup (Gen. xv. 16). His own education was very incomplete; it would take at least forty years to drain him of his self-will and self-reliance, and make him a vessel meet for the Master's use. The Hebrew people had not as yet come to the pitch of anguish, which is so touchingly referred to, when the death of their principal oppressor seems to have brought matters to a crisis, and they forsook the false gods to which they had given their allegiance in order to return to the God of their fathers (Exod. ii. 23).

We all know something of this haste. We find it so hard to sit still, whilst our great Boaz does his work (Ruth. iii. 18). We think that the set time of God's salvation must have arrived, long before the clock strikes. As Saul, in presence of the Philistine invasion, we suppose that we cannot last out for another hour, and force ourselves to offer the burnt-offering; and are chagrined to see Samuel's figure slowly pacing up the mountain pass as the fire burns down to its last embers, and to hear from his lips the sentence of deposition for our impatience (1 Sam. xiii. 12–14). Well may our Master say of us, as He did once of his brethren, "My time is not yet come; but your time is alway ready" (John vii. 6).

Oh for grace to wait and watch with God, though a horror of

great darkness fall on us, and sleep steals up into our eyes, and the head becomes thickly sown with the grey hair of age ! One blow struck when the time is fulfilled is worth a thousand struck in premature eagerness. It is not for thee, O my soul, to know the times and seasons which the Father hath put in his own power; wait thou only upon God; let thy expectation be from Him; wait at the gates of thy Jericho for yet seven days; utter not a sound till He says, Shout: but when He gives the signal, with the glad cry of victory thou shalt pass over the fallen wall into the city.

(3) *It was executed in the pride of human strength.* It was but natural that Moses should suppose that he could do something for the amelioration of his people's lot. He had always been accustomed to have his way. Crowds of obsequious servants and courtiers had yielded to his slightest whim. By his strong right hand he had hewn out a great career. He was conscious of vast stores of youthful energy and natural force, untapped by sufficient calls, and undiminished by physical excess; surely these would count for something. He would make that nation of oppressors reel before his blows, and of course he would be hailed by his brethren as their God-sent deliverer.

It was a rude surprise when, on the second day, he went out to continue his self-imposed task, and essayed to adjust a difference between two Hebrews, to find himself repulsed from them by the challenge, "Who made thee a prince and a judge over us ?" He had never expected a rebuff from that quarter. "For he supposed his brethren would have understood how that God, by his hand, would deliver them: but they understood not." Evidently, then, God's time had not arrived; nor could it come until the heat of his spirit had slowly evaporated in the desert air, and he had learnt the hardest of all lessons, that "by strength shall no man prevail."

We have been disposed to attribute too much of the success of the Exodus to the natural qualities of the great leader; but we must always remember that, like Gideon's host, he was at first too strong for God. God cannot give his glory to another. He dare not entrust his power to men, till they are humbled and emptied, and conscious of their helplessness. Even the Son learned obedience by the things that He suffered, and descended into the dust of death, crying, "I am a worm and no man," ere He could say, "All power is given unto Me in heaven and in earth." The most eminent of his saints must suffer from a thorn in the flesh, to remind him of his weakness; and he confessed himself grateful for it, because only when he was weak could he be strong. When the soul is inflated with a strong reliance on its own sufficiency, the power of God is unable to effect an entrance, or use that soul as a channel for its work. It is when we are willing to be accounted as worms, as broken reeds, as little children, as foolish, weak, base, despised, as "things which are not," that we become aware of being vehicles for the working of the might of his power, which He wrought in Christ when He raised Him from the dead. You must be brought to an end of yourself before God can begin with you. But when once you have come to that point there is no limit to what may be wrought during a single life by the passage through it of his eternal power and God-head.

(4) *It was too apprehensive of the judgment of other men.* We are told that he looked this way and that way before he smote the Egyptian; and when he found that his deed of revenge was known, he feared and fled (Exod. ii. 15). But suppose that he had felt that he had been divinely commissioned to execute judgment upon Egypt; suppose he had realized the Divine Presence with him; suppose he had known that he was on the line of Divine purpose—would he have cared who was looking, and what was being said? It would not have been possible. Fixing his eyes on the movement of the Divine cloud, absorbed in the one passion of doing God's will, sure that he was immortal till his work was done, he would have been perfectly indifferent to the praise or blame of men. Whenever men look this way and that to see what other men are doing or saying, you may be quite sure that they do not know certainly their Master's plan; they are in front of Him, and are acting from the prompting of their own self-will, though perhaps under the cover of religious zeal.

There has been only one perfect Servant of God who has ever trodden our world. He never looked this way nor that. Away on the mountain height of unbroken fellowship He received the plan of his life, which He wrought out in daily detail, and He alone could say, "He that sent Me is with Me; the Father hath not left Me alone, for I do always those things that please Him." Oh for the single eye, that our whole body also may be full of light !

II. THE FLIGHT TO THE DESERT.—The news of Moses' first attempt came to the ears of Pharaoh, and he sought to slay Moses. But Moses feared, and fled from the face of Pharaoh. In after years, under similar circumstances, it is said, "He forsook Egypt, not fearing the wrath of the king" (Heb. xi. 27). And when we ask the reason of his fearlessness, we learn that it was by faith he did so; for "he endured, as seeing Him who is invisible." But if such were the case afterwards, why was it not so at the time with which we are dealing? Why did he not exercise faith in the invisible God? Why did not his heart beat with even throb in the one crisis as in the other. The reason is obvious.

Faith is only possible when we are on God's plan, and stand on God's promise. It is useless to pray for increased faith until we have fulfilled the conditions of faith. It is equally useless to spend time in regrets and tears over the failures which are due to our unbelief. "And the Lord said to Joshua, Get thee up; wherefore liest thou thus upon thy face?" Faith is as natural to right conditions of soul, as a flower is to a plant. And amongst those conditions this is the first—ascertain your place in God's plan, and get on to it; and this is the second—feed on God's promises. And when each of these is realized, faith comes of itself; and there is absolutely nothing which is impossible. The believing soul can "do all things" with God, because it has got on to God's lines; yea, it is itself as the metal track along which God travels to men in love, grace, and truth.

But Moses was out of touch with God. So he fled, and crossed the desert that lay between him and the eastern frontier; threaded the mountain passes of the Sinaitic peninsula, through which in after years he was to lead his people; and at last sat wearily down by a well in the land of Midian. There his chivalrous interference was suddenly elicited on behalf of the daughters of the priest of Midian, who seem to have suffered daily from the insolence of shepherds appropriating the water which the shepherd-maidens had drawn for their flocks. That day, however, the churls met their match, and were compelled to leave the water-troughs to the women; who hurried home, unexpectedly early, to tell, with girls' enthusiasm, of the Egyptian who had delivered them from the hand of the shepherds. It was a good office that could not pass without requital in that hospitable land, and it opened the door to the chieftain's tent; ultimately to marriage with one of those same shepherdesses; and finally to the quiet life of a shepherd in the calm open spaces of that wonderful land, which, on more than one occasion, has served for a Divine school.

Such experiences come to us all. We rush forward, thinking to carry all before us; we strike a few blows in vain; we are staggered with disappointment, and reel back; we are afraid at the first breath of human disapprobation; we flee from the scenes of our discomfiture to hide ourselves in chagrin. Then we are hidden in the secret of God's presence from the pride of man. And there our vision clears: the silt drops from the current of our life, as from the Rhone in its passage through the deep waters of Geneva's lake; our self-life dies down; our spirit drinks of the river of God, which is full of water; our faith begins to grasp his arm, and to be the channel for the manifestation of his power; and thus at last we emerge to be his hand to lead an Exodus. "This also cometh forth from the Lord of hosts, who is wonderful in counsel, and excellent in working."

V

The Marvellous Colloquy

"God called unto him out of the midst of the bush, and said Moses,
Moses. And he said, Here am I."
—Exod. iii. 4.

A Memorable Day.—There are days in all lives which come unannounced, unheralded; no angel faces look out of heaven; no angel voices put us on our guard: but as we look back on them in after years, we realize that they were the turning points of existence. Perhaps we look longingly back on the uneventful routine of the life that lies beyond them; but the angel, with drawn sword, forbids our return, and compels us forward. It was so with Moses.

Quite ordinary was that morning as it broke. The sun rose as usual in a dull haze over the expanse of sand, or above the gaunt forms of the mountains, seamed and scarred. As the young day opened, it began to shine in a cloudless sky, casting long shadows over the plains; and presently, climbing to the zenith, threw a searching, scorching light into every aperture of the landscape beneath. The sheep browsed as usual on the scant herbage, or lay panting beneath the shadow of a great rock; but there was nothing in their behaviour to excite the thought that God was nigh. The giant forms of the mountains, the spreading heavens, the awful silence unbroken by song of bird or hum of insect life, the acacia bushes drooping in the shadeless glare—these things were as they had been for forty years, and as they threatened to be, after Moses had sunk into an obscure and forgotten grave. Then, all suddenly, a common bush began to shine with the emblem of Deity; and from its heart of fire the voice of God broke the silence of the ages in words that fell on the shepherd's ear like a double-knock: "Moses, Moses."

And from that moment all his life was altered. The door which had been so long in repairing was suddenly put on its hinges again

33

and opened. The peaceful quiet, the meditative leisure, the hiding from the strife of tongues, the simple piety of the homestead—where the priest of Midian ministered, and Zipporah welcomed him with his boys, as he brought the flock home to its fold—suddenly vanished, as a tract of land submerged beneath the ocean. And he went forth, not clearly knowing whither; knowing only that he dared not be disobedient to the heavenly vision, or refuse the voice of Him that spake.

That voice still speaks to those whose hearts are hushed to hear. By written letter or printed page, by the beauty of a holy life, the spell of some precious memory, or the voice of some living teacher, the God of past generations still makes known his will to the anointed ear. Nor will our lives ever be what they might until we realize that God has a plan for every hour in them; and that He waits to reveal that plan to the loving and obedient heart, making it known to us by one of the ten thousand ministries that lie around us. Insensibly to ourselves we contract the habit of thinking of Him as the God of the dead, who spake to the fathers in oracle and prophet; whereas the I AM is God of the living—passing through our crowded thoroughfares, brooding over our desert spaces, and seeking hearts which are still enough from their own plannings and activities to listen.

The main point for each of us is to be able to answer his summons with the response, "Here am I." It may seem long to wait, and the oft-expected day so slow in coming, that the heart sinks down, oppressed with the crowd of common days, and relinquishes hope; but your opportunity will come at last. Be always ready ! Never let the loins be ungirded, or the lamps expire; never throw yourself down at full length by the brook, to drink lazily of the limpid stream. In such an hour as you think not the Lord will come. What rapture to be able to answer his appeal with, "Here am I." If that summons were to come to-day, too many of us would have to ask for a moment's respite while we went to finish some neglected duty. Oh for the free, untrammelled, unengaged spirit, to be ready to go at any moment whithersoever the Lord may appoint.

A REMARKABLE ANNOUNCEMENT.—Out of the bush came the voice of God, blending past, present, and future, in one marvellous sentence: *the past*, "I am the God of thy father, the God of Abraham, the God of Isaac, and the God of Jacob"; *the present*, "I have surely seen the affliction of my people which are in Egypt, and have heard their cry by reason of their taskmasters; for I know their sorrows, and I am come down to deliver them"; *the future*, "Come now, therefore, and I will send thee unto Pharaoh" (Exod. iii. 6–10).

Deep and searching thoughts arrest us, which should be laid most seriously to heart, especially by the Lord's busiest workers. We are all too apt to run before we are sent, as Moses did in his first well-meant, but ill-timed, endeavours. We put our hands, at our own prompting, to a work that needs doing; we ask God to help us, and we go on very well with the momentum of our own energy for at least a day. But on the morrow, when chiding and rebuke and difficulty arise, as they did to Moses, we are disappointed, and throw it all up; betaking ourselves to flight, finding our refuge in the solitudes of the desert.

But what a contrast to all this ineffectual effort and dismal disappointment is presented in those who have learnt to wait for God! When the time is full, they hear Him say, *I am come down, and I will send thee*; and from that moment they are no longer promoters, but instruments, agents, and tools, through whom He executes his plans. What, then, are difficulties to them? They anticipate them without anxiety; they pass through them without fear. God must have foreseen all before He put his hand to the work. He must be able to see a pathway threading the apparently trackless waste. He must know a door through what appears to be an impregnable barrier of rock. At any rate, the chosen soul has simply to walk with Him; to be ready to do the errands He requires, whether they consist in accosting monarchs, lifting up a rod, or uttering his words. That is all; and then to stand still to watch the ease with which He cleaves a pathway through the sea, and provides a commissariat in the desert.

DIVINE LONG-SUFFERING UNDER PROVOCATION.—In the first blush of youthful enthusiasm Moses had been impetuous enough to attempt the emancipation of his people by the blows of his right hand. But now that God proposes to send him to lead an Exodus, he starts back in dismay almost petrified at the proposal. But how true this is to nature! The student, as a precocious schoolboy, thinks that he knows all that can be acquired of a certain branch of science; but twenty years after he feels as if he had not mastered its elements, though he has never ceased to study. The believer who began by speaking of himself as "the least of saints" ends by calling himself "the chief of sinners." And Moses, who had run before God in feverish impatience, now lags faint-hearted behind Him.

At first he expostulated: "Who am I, that I should go to Pharaoh?" There was something more than humility here; there was a tone of self-depreciation which was inconsistent with a true faith in God's selection and appointment. Surely it is God's business to choose his special instruments; and when we are persuaded that we are in the line of his purpose, we have no right to question the wisdom of his appointment. To do so is to depreciate his wisdom, or to doubt his power and willingness to become the complement of our need.

"And God said, Certainly, I will be with thee." "I whose glory shines here, who am as unimpaired by the flight of the ages as this fire is by burning; who am independent of sustenance or fuel from man; who made the fathers what they were; whose nature is incapable of change—I will be with thee." What an assurance was here ! And yet something of this kind is said to each of us when we are called to undertake any new charge. We have been called into the fellowship of the Son of God. "He died for us, that whether we wake or sleep, we should live together with Him." He is with us all the days, even unto the end of the age. He will never leave us, neither forsake us. "Fear not," He seems to say; "I am with thee: I who change not, and without whom no sparrow falls to the ground. All power is given unto Me in heaven and in earth. Not an hour without my companionship; not a difficulty without my co-operation; not a Red Sea without my right arm; not a mile of wilderness journeying without the Angel of my Presence." Days break very differently on us. Sometimes we open the door to a flood of sunshine, sometimes to a sky laden with black, dull clouds; now a funeral, and then a marriage; hours in which it is luxury to live, and others which pass with leaden-footed pace; but nothing can part us from our Divine Companion—nothing but needless worry or permitted sin.

In his next excuse Moses professed his inability to answer if he were asked the name of God (13); and this was met by the proclamation of the spirit-stirring name, JEHOVAH: I AM THAT I AM. There we have the unity of God to the exclusion of the many gods of Egypt; the unchangeableness of God, who lives in an eternal present; the self-sufficiency of God, who alone is his own equivalent.

No other term can describe Him; when you have said your utmost you must fall back on this—that God is God.

The term JEHOVAH was not wholly unknown to Moses, for it entered into his mother's name, Jochebed—*Jehovah my glory*; but now for the first time it was adopted as the unique title by which God was to be known in Israel. Slowly it made its way into the faith of the people; and whenever employed, it speaks of the self-existent and redeeming qualities of the nature of God, and is for ever enshrined in the precious name of our Saviour, JESUS. The whole subsequent life of Moses and of Israel was inspired by this name. All through their history the thought of what He was, and what He would be to them, rang out like a chime of bells.

And for us it is full of meaning. "This," said He, "is my name for ever, and this is my memorial to all generations" (15). And as its full meaning opens to our vision, it is as if God put into our hands a blank cheque, leaving us to fill it in as we will. Are we dark ? let us add to his I AM the words, *the true Light*; are we hungry ? the words, *the Bread of Life*; are we defenceless ? the words, *the Good Shepherd*; are we weary? the words, *Shiloh, the Rest-giver.* "In Him dwelleth all the fulness of the Godhead bodily, and in Him ye are made full" (Col. ii. 9, 10, R.V.).

Moses' third excuse was that the people would not believe him, nor hearken to his voice (Exod. iv. 1). But God graciously met this also by showing him miracles which he might perform in Egypt, and which would read deep lessons to himself. "What is that in thine hand ? And he said, A rod." It was probably only a shepherd's crook. What a history, however, awaited it ! It was to be stretched out over the Red Sea, pointing a pathway through its depths; to smite the flinty rock; to win victory over the hosts of Amalek; to be known as the Rod of God. When God wants an implement for his service He does not choose the golden sceptre, but a shepherd's crook; the weakest and meanest thing He can find—a ram's horn, a cake of barley meal, an ox-goad, an earthen pitcher, a shepherd's sling. He employs a worm to thresh the mountains and make the hills as chaff. A rod with God behind it is mightier than the vastest army.

At God's command the rod was cast on the ground, and it became a serpent. In Egyptian worship the serpent played a very conspicuous part. And as it wriggled on the sand, and sought to do him harm, so that he fled from it, it was an emblem of the might of Egypt before which he had become a fugitive. But, when God gave the word, how easily it became once more a rod in his hand, as he fearlessly grasped the venomous animal by the tail. So God would instruct his faith. If only he would dare to do as he was bidden, Pharaoh and all his priests, and the whole force of the Egyptian empire would be equally submissive.

The second sign was even more significant. His hand thrust into his bosom became leprous; and then again pure and white. It was as if God met his consciousness of moral pollution, and taught him that it could be put away as easily as his flesh was cleansed through His forgiving grace.

And the third sign, in which it was promised that the water of the Nile should become blood on the dry land, was full of terrible omen to the gods of that mighty country, the people of which depended so entirely on its river, and worshipped it as a god.

We may well ponder these significant signs. Are we only as rods, and rods which were once serpents ? Yet God can do great things by us, if only we are willing to be wielded by his hand. Are we polluted with the leprosy of sin ? Yet we may be as his hand, thrust into his bosom and made clean and pure. Are our foes many ? They are his foes too, absolutely in his power to cover them with confusion.

The last excuse that Moses alleged was his lack of eloquence. "O Lord, I am not eloquent; I am slow of speech, and of a slow tongue" (ver. 10). Probably, like our Cromwell, he had no ready supply of words. But God was willing to meet this also with his patient grace; and if only Moses had been willing to trust Him, it is probable that he would have added the gifts of a persuasive and splendid oratory to the other talents with which he was so copiously endowed. "And the Lord said, Who hath made man's mouth ? or who maketh the dumb, or deaf, or the seeing, or the blind ? Have not I, the Lord ? Now therefore go, and I will be with thy mouth, and teach thee what thou shalt say" (verses 11, 12).

But Moses would not believe it; so at length the Divine anger burnt against him, and the Lord ended the conference by saying that He would send Aaron with him, to be his colleague and spokesman. Ah ! better a thousand times had it been for him to trust God for speech, than be thus deposed from his premiership ! Aaron shaped the golden calf, and wrought folly in Israel, and became a thorn in the side of the saint of God. And probably in the eyes of their contemporaries, Aaron engrossed the greater attention, and had most of the honour and credit of the great deliverance.

THE FINAL ASSENT.—It was a very grudging one. "And he said, O my Lord, send, I pray Thee, by the hand of him whom Thou wilt send." It was as much as to say, "Since Thou art determined to send me, and I must undertake the mission, then let it be so; but I would that it might have been another, and I go because I am compelled." So often do we shrink back from the sacrifice or obligation to which God calls us, that we think we are going to our doom. We seek every reason for evading the Divine will, little realizing that He is forcing us out from our quiet homes into a career which includes, among other things, the song of victory on the banks of the Red Sea; the two lonely sojourns for forty days in converse with God; the shining face; the vision of glory; the burial by the hand of Michael; and the supreme honour of standing beside the Lord on the Transfiguration Mount.

VI

" To Egypt "

"And Moses returned to the land of Egypt; and took the rod of
God in his hand."
—Exod. iv. 20.

THE FIRE faded from the bush; the light above the brightness of the
sun died away; the voice was still; and Moses looked around on the
browsing sheep and the mighty mountains with the strange wonder
of a man awaking from a trance. It had been the supreme hour of
his life; for which all previous years had been preparing, and from
which all future ones would date.

I. FIRST STEPS TOWARD RETURN.—Slowly, thoughtfully, perhaps
painfully, he prepared to obey the heavenly summons. Gathering
his flock together, he conducted it from the backside of the desert,
with its stern grandeur, its unoccupied spaces, its intense silence, to
Midian, the seat of his clan, where human voices and interests could
reassert themselves. "And Moses went and returned to Jethro, his
father-in-law." By inter-marriage with the tribe of which Jethro was
the chieftain, Moses had placed himself under those olden customs
which still obtain, as unchanged as the world of nature around them,
among the wild sons of the desert. One of these customs demanded
that any member of the tribe should seek and obtain permission
before starting on a distant errand, involving prolonged absence
from the camp. This permission Moses sought. "Let me go, I pray
thee, and return unto my brethren which are in Egypt, and see
whether they be yet alive."

Probably he said nothing of the vision he had seen, or of the
mission with which he had been entrusted; and it was a noble
reserve. We conserve spiritual strength when we refrain from
speaking of our dealings with the Lord. Of course it is sometimes
necessary to speak of them, to explain our reasons for action or to
lead other souls into the same experiences; but it takes the freshness

and delicacy from our inner fellowship with God if we are always talking about it. It is not the nature of the deepest love to unveil all its endearments to unsympathizing eyes. It is much more important that men should see and feed on the fruits and results of such intercourse, than that they should be admitted to study its inner secrets. So Moses only sought leave to depart by the way which he had come some forty years before.

The request must have involved surprise and pain to the entire family. They never suspected that strong heart of yearnings for the distant land where his kinsfolk were slaves. He seemed to have become so entirely one with themselves. And his going would involve that of wife and boys and of the infant son, who seems to have been but recently born. However, no obstacle was thrown in his way, and the permission he asked was granted in the laconic answer, "Go in peace."

But even then he lingered. So utterly had the forty years done their work, that his impulsive, hasty spirit had died down; and he who previously had run before God now began to lag behind Him. He was in no hurry to be gone. Was it that he dreaded the turmoil and stir of the busy crowds of those teeming hives of population? Was it that he had commenced to feel the pressure of growing years, disinclining him from great exertion? Was it that he loved the hush of those desert solitudes, and the companionship of those mighty mountains, and was reluctant to tear himself away from them? Was it that he had misgivings about the safety of his person when exposed to the hatred of king and court? We cannot tell the reason; our only point is to notice the marvellous transformation which had been wrought in his inner life, the deliberation, the self-possession, the reserve. For these qualities were so in the ascendant that it was needful for God to send a second summons into his life. "And the Lord said unto Moses in Midian: Go, return into Egypt; for all the men are dead which sought thy life."

Stirred up by this second summons, as Abraham by the second summons—which came to him also—when Terah was dead, Moses prepared to start for Egypt. It was a very simple cavalcade, reminding us of another which, in similar lowliness, but centuries after, was destined to travel through a part of that same desert towards the same goal. Moses, however, went as the servant who was faithful in all his house; but the infant whom Mary carried was the Son who had builded the house, and was coming to live in it for ever.

Imagine, then, that setting-forth. Zipporah sitting on the ass, perhaps nursing a little babe, new-born, whilst the husband and father walked beside. And in his hand was the sacred rod—only a shepherd's crook, but now the rod of God—destined to be employed for deeds of transcendent power, and always reminding him of what weak things could do when wielded by strong hands behind them. Three things happened on that journey.

II. A FURTHER REVELATION.—"And the Lord said unto Moses, . . ." (21). And there followed a marvellous epitome of events which were to transpire within the next few months, from the making of the water into blood to the slaying of the first-born.

This was in harmony with one of the greatest principles in the moral and spiritual realm. We only learn as we endeavour to obey. Light is given to us to know what next step we should take—just light enough and no more; a rim of light, hemmed in by darkness falling as a faint circle on our path. Shall we take that step? We hesitate, because we cannot see the step beyond, and the next beyond; or because we fail to see the reason, and are not satisfied to act on the conviction of known duty; or because we dread the awful pain which threatens to benumb us and turn our hearts sick. But so long as we refuse to act, that light cannot increase, but begins inevitably to decline. Obedience is the one condition for its increase, nay, for its maintenance at all.

It may be that you are in darkness like that which enveloped King Saul towards the end of his troubled reign, when the Lord answered him not, "neither by dreams, nor by Urim, nor by prophets." It is long since you heard his voice, or saw his face. But as with Saul so with you, disobedience is the cause. You have neglected to perform the Divine commandments; you have disobeyed the distinct word of the Lord. And you will never get back into the warm, blessed, circle of his manifested presence, where his face smiles and his voice speaks, till you have gone back to the place where you dropped the thread of obedience, and, taking it up where you left it, do what you know to be the word and will of God. Then, as you start to obey, the voice of God will greet you once more with the old familiar tones.

III. A PREPARATORY RITE.—In the caravanserai Moses seems to have been attacked by sudden and dangerous illness, and was on the

point of death. What a strange and awful visitation!—that the
destined deliverer of Israel should die amid the hubbub and unrest
of an Eastern Khan; his call cancelled; his wife returning to her
people, a widow; his children fatherless; his people unenfranchised.
But amid the horror of that hour conscience did its work unmolested,
and searched the secrets of his heart with her lighted torch. How
often have we experienced a similar dealing at the Lord's hands!
We have lain all night in a bath of fire; we have suffered almost to
the limits of sanity; we have gone down to the depths of the ocean of
grief: and as we have raised our weary eyes to God, and asked the
reason of discipline so searching, his answer has come back to us in
the memory of some hidden sin or neglected duty.

It would seem that for some reason Moses had neglected the rite
of circumcision for one of his children, perhaps the newly-born one.
That reason may have been due to Zipporah's dislike. He allowed
her to have her way; but, as the head of the house, he was held
responsible for its omission. We cannot shirk responsibilities placed
on our shoulders by God Himself. The husband cannot put them
on the wife, nor the wife take them from the husband. And as he
seemed to hang in the quivering balance, between life and death,
this was brought to mind, and he was compelled to insist that the rite
should be performed.

It was comparatively a trivial thing, insignificant in the eyes of
man; and yet there are no trifles in a man's dealings with God.
Great principles are involved in very insignificant acts, as ponderous
bridges revolve on very small pivots. The self-life is sometimes more
strongly intrenched in a small thing than in a bigger one. And so
he is kept waiting on the threshold of the great enterprise of his life,
because this rite of circumcision had not been administered to a
little babe. We may be conscious of having been sent to do a great
work for God, and yet be shrinking from some small known duty;
and disobedience here will impede our progress, as the stone in a
traveller's shoe. We can never learn the lesson too deeply, that our
action in the commonplaces of life is deciding our destiny. What
we are in them will affect all our future, making us either the
emancipators of our people, or carcases that bleach on the desert
sand.

There is a very striking passage in the Minor Prophets, in which
God says, "You only have I known of all the families of the earth;
therefore I will punish you for all your iniquities" (Amos iii. 2).

The more dear we are to God, the more care will He expend on us. The more fruit-bearing qualities we possess, the more thoroughly shall we be pruned. The finest, rarest, metals are exposed to the whitest heat. And it was because Moses was to be so eminently used, that he came into God's most searching discipline. Take heart, suffering child of God ! He chastens because He loves, and is about to use you. Be careful to ascertain the evil thing which grieves Him, and put it away; or if it seem impossible to put it out of thy life, ask the Priest to cut it out, for, though touched with our pain, He holds a sharp two-edged sword to pierce to the very border-land of soul and spirit. Then shall God remove the stroke of his hand. "So He let him go."

The exhibition of incompatibility displayed by Zipporah, when she had performed the rite, seems to have led Moses to feel that it would not be wise to take her with him; and, on the whole, it seemed better that she should abide quietly with her own people, until the act of emancipation was wrought. And this was easier, inasmuch as God had so distinctly told him that he should bring the people through those very districts on their way to Canaan (Exod. iii. 12). And it befell according to his faith; for in the after narrative we find this record, "Jethro, Moses' father-in-law, came with his sons and his wife unto Moses into the wilderness, where he encamped at the mount of God" (Exod. xviii. 5).

We are not always to follow this example in ridding ourselves of family ties in order to do God's work. At the same time, a man must always move steadily forward on the appointed plan of his life, not swayed by, but swaying, the members of his home, and bearing them along with him in one common work. The circumstances must be very exceptional that invade the close ties of the home; but when such circumstances arise, they will be so evidently indicated by God's providence that there will be no reflection cast on the character of his servants.

IV. A BROTHERLY ALLIANCE.—Recovered from his illness, but lonely, Moses, having sent back his wife and children, started again on his journey, threading his way through those corridors of red sandstone, by which he had passed some forty years ago. But how different all seemed ! *He* was different. No longer a disappointed man, smarting with the sense of recent failure; but strong in the Lord, and in the power of his might, conscious of a great mission, and of the presence of an angel beside him who would be equal to every emergency.

And he knew that the same power which brought him forward was bringing towards him the brother whom he had not seen for forty years. How the hearts of the two throbbed at the thought of meeting ! How eagerly would each press forward ! How earnestly would each scan the distant figure of the other in the long vista ! And, finally, God so contrived it that they met in the Mount of God, where the bush had burned, and the voice of God had summoned Moses from shepherding a flock to become shepherd of a host. Then what greetings ! "He kissed him." What interchange of confidences! "Moses told Aaron all the words of the Lord who had sent him." What questionings, as the exile would ask tidings of those whom he had loved !

So we shall meet. God knows where our Aarons are, our twin-souls whom we need to have beside us for the completion of our life-work. They may be far away now. But He is bringing them to us, and us to them. The Zipporah goes, but the Aaron comes. And we shall not miss each other, since He is guide. Let us live on his providence and love; and He will so arrange it finally that we shall meet at the Mount of God, some consecrated spot, some bower of holy converse, some blessed trysting-place, selected by Himself. And the embrace, the joy, the kiss of welcome, shall in the ecstasy cause us to forget the forty years of exile, loneliness, and sorrow.

VII

Failure and Disappointment

"And Moses said, Lord, wherefore hast Thou so evil entreated this people ? why is it that Thou hast sent me ? For since I came to Pharaoh to speak in Thy name, he hath done evil to this people; neither hast Thou delivered Thy people at all."
—Exod. v. 22, 23.

In loving interchange of thought, the noble and venerable brothers reached Egypt; and in pursuance of the Divine command proceeded to summon the elders of Israel to a conference, at which they should present their credentials, and give utterance to the Divine message with which they were entrusted.

I. The Interview with the Elders.—It must have been a very remarkable meeting, perhaps the first of the sort ever held. Never before had this downtrodden nation produced men daring enough to take such a step, the first, indeed, towards national autonomy. We are not told whether there was any disposition on the part of any of these elders, who were probably the heads of the Hebrew families and tribes, to question the right of the brothers to convene them. In all likelihood, they were but too glad to merge all prior and selfish claims in a united effort on their people's behalf; and there were probably many stories afloat of Moses' life and deeds, before his strange and sudden self-expatriation, which predisposed them to obey his call, and gather at some convenient spot within the territory allotted to them to inhabit.

When all were gathered Aaron recited on the behalf of Moses, who probably stood beside him without a word, the magnificent words spoken at the bush (Exod. iii. 16–22). We do not know how they were received. Perhaps Moses' own fear was partly realized when he said to God, "They will not believe me, nor hearken unto my voice; for they will say, the Lord hath not appeared unto thee."

The long years of bondage may have so quenched their hopes and quelled their spirits that they were unable to realize that the hour of deliverance had come. As the inmates of the house of Mary could not believe that Peter, for whose release they had been praying, really stood outside the door; so it was almost impossible to believe that the days of slavery were nearly ended, and that the hands of the clock of their destiny were at last pointing to the hour of release.

At this juncture the brothers would probably give the signs with which God had provided them: the serpent changed into a rod; the leprous hand made natural and whole; the water of the river becoming blood as it was poured out upon the land (Exod. iv. 2–9). These won conviction; and from that meeting the tidings spread throughout the nation, whispered from hut to hut, told in under-breaths from slave to slave among the brick-kilns. "And the people believed; and when they heard that the Lord had visited the children of Israel, and that He had looked upon their affliction, then they bowed their heads and worshipped."

II. THE AUDIENCE WITH PHARAOH.—The next point for the brothers was to go to Pharaoh, with the demand that he should let the people go to hold a feast in the wilderness. This was according to the Divine direction (Exod. iii. 18); and was moreover a reasonable request. So fastidious a people as the Egyptians could well understand how Israel would prefer to carry out their rites apart from the inspection of strangers, and the contagion of the predominant religious cult surrounding them. Besides, it was like asking for a brief holiday, after an unbroken spell of centuries of incessant toil. It did not set forth all they wanted; but inasmuch as it was a foregone conclusion that Pharaoh would grant nothing, every care was taken to deprive him of the excuse of saying that their demands were preposterous.

It was probably in an audience-room of some splendid palace, where the lordly Pharaoh received deputations and embassies, that they met him. How mixed must Moses' feelings have been, entering as a suppliant the precincts in which he had played no inconspicuous part in those buried years! And then Aaron and he uttered the words, which pealed as a thunder-clap through the audience, "Thus saith the Lord God of Israel, Let my people go, that they may hold a feast unto Me in the wilderness."

In order to appreciate the audacity of the demand, we must remember the unbridled power and authority which were claimed by the Egyptian monarchs. Each Pharaoh was the child of the sun. He is depicted as fondled by the greatest gods, and sitting with them in the recesses of their temples to receive worship equal to their own. "By the life of Pharaoh," was the supreme oath. Without Pharaoh could no man lift up his hand or foot in all the land of Egypt. For him great Egypt existed. For him all other men lived, suffered, and died. For him the mighty Nile flowed from its unexplored fountains to fructify the soil. For him vast armies of priests, and magicians, and courtiers, wrought and ministered. From his superb throne he looked down on the wretched crowds of subject peoples, careless of their miseries. What were their tears and groans, and the wail of their bondage, but a fitting sacrifice to be offered to his exalted majesty! In addition, the present monarch had recently, through his generals, achieved certain great victories; and these successes had greatly enhanced his arrogant pride, so that it was in a paroxysm of supercilious scorn that he answered the Divine demand: "Who is the Lord, that I should obey his voice, to let Israel go? I know not the Lord, neither will I let Israel go."

The point of the reply lies in that word *obey*. He saw that these men did not present him with a request, but with a mandate from One of greater authority than himself. This stung him to the quick. He also was a god. Who was this other God, stronger than himself, who dared to issue such a summons! A God of whose existence till that moment he had been unaware! The God of a parcel of slaves! How dare they speak of their paltry Deity in his presence, and in the midst of priests, courtiers, and high officers of state!

The brothers met this outburst with a reiteration of their message, telling how the God of the Hebrews had met with them; and requesting, in a softer tone, that they might be permitted to do as He had enjoined. But the king refused to believe that their plea was genuine; and insisted on regarding the whole matter as a desire to escape from their labours, and as a plea for idleness. Turning sharply on the two brethren, he accused them of hindering their people's toils, and bade them begone to their own share in the clay-pit, or the brick-kiln: "Wherefore do ye, Moses and Aaron, let the people from their works? Get you unto your burdens." What a bitter taunt there was in that last sentence! How the royal lip curled as it was uttered! Already the heart had begun to harden! And so the audience ended, and the brothers came down the crowded corridors amid the titter of the court. A very different scene was to be enacted a few months later, as the news came there of the overthrow of the monarch in the Red Sea—the last stage of the conflict between himself and the God of the Hebrews, whose name he heard that day for the first time.

III. FAILURE AND DISAPPOINTMENT.—That same day a new order was issued from the palace, emanating from Pharaoh himself, to the taskmasters of the people. And probably, ere the evening fell, the ominous word had passed from the taskmasters to the head-men who were set over their fellow Hebrews, and were, therefore, responsible for the daily delivery of a certain tale of bricks, that they must expect no more straw, though the daily returns must be maintained. "Thus saith Pharaoh, I will not give you straw; go ye, get you straw where ye can find it. Yet not aught of your work shall be diminished."

Then ensued a time of awful anguish. The Hebrew head-men told off some of the people to scatter themselves over the country, collecting straw from every quarter, and to do it with all haste. And in the meantime they urged on the rest of the people to compensate for the absence of the straw-gatherers by their added energy. Every nerve was strained to the uttermost. From early morning to the last ray of light the whole nation sought to do the impossible beneath the scorching sun, and with never a moment's pause. And yet as the tale of bricks was counted it fell inevitably short. In vain did the taskmasters haste them, saying, "Fulfil your works, your daily tasks, as when there was straw." In vain were the officers of the children of Israel, whom Pharaoh's taskmasters had set over them, beaten, and such beating as they would get might mean death. It was as when a whole crew, stripped to the waist, works at the pumps; but they cannot pump out the water as quickly as it pours in; the water-line will not fall, and at length drowning is preferable to the agonized suspense.

Finally, they could stand it no longer, and resolved to make an appeal direct to Pharaoh. "The officers of the children of Israel came and cried unto Pharaoh" (ver. 15). It was a bitter day for the two brothers when the people took the matter into their own hands, and, without using them as intermediaries, went direct to the king to get him to put them back to the point at which they stood before that well-meant, but disastrous interference. But it was evidently better that Moses and Aaron should wait outside the palace to learn the result of the interview (ver. 20).

It happened just as it might have been expected, the king would not listen to the appeal made to him. "He said, Ye are idle, ye are idle: therefore ye say, Let us go and do sacrifice to the Lord. Go therefore now, and work; for there shall no straw be given to you, yet shall ye deliver the tale of bricks" (verses 17, 18). It may be that he referred again sarcastically to the "vain words," on which the brothers had caused them to hope (ver. 9). And so they came forth from Pharaoh, at the very extreme of agony, dreading the lingering death from exhaustion and stripes, which apparently awaited their whole nation; and as Moses and Aaron stood there they poured on them the bitterness of their spirit. What must it not have been for them to hear from those lips the bitterest reproaches they could frame, cutting them as knives, although they would have gladly given their lives to alleviate the circumstances out of which they sprang?—"The Lord look upon you, and judge; because ye have made our savour to stink in the eyes of Pharaoh, and in the eyes of his servants, to put a sword into their hand to slay us."

As we look back on that scene, we can somewhat understand the reason for it all. God can afford to bring us through passages like this, because of "the afterward" to which they lead. It was necessary that Moses, Aaron, and the Hebrews, should come to see that their case was desperate, and that no appeals or reasonings or remonstrances could alter it. It was necessary that the leaders should be weaned from the enthusiastic loyalty of the people, that they might lean only on the arm of the living God, and venture forth depending on Him alone. It was necessary that the people should see that they could not better their position by any efforts of their own. Yes, and their thoughts would henceforth be directed past the leaders, who were discredited in their very first endeavour, to the hand and heart of the Almighty.

IV. THE RESORT OF THE BAFFLED SOUL.—"And Moses returned unto the Lord, and said, Lord, wherefore hast thou so evil entreated this people? Why is it that Thou hast sent me?" (ver. 22). There is no other help for us when passing through such stern discipline; and the man who cannot flee thither in similar straits is pitiable indeed. When we see our hopes blasted, our plans miscarry, our efforts do more harm than good, whilst we are discredited and blamed, pursued with the taunts and hate of those for whom we were willing to lay down our lives, we may preserve an outward calm; but there will be a heart-break underneath, and the noblest part in us will wither, as corn blasted by an east wind, unless we are able to pour out our whole complaint before God.

The agony of soul through which Moses passed must have been as death to him. He died to his self-esteem, to his castle-building, to pride in his miracles, to the enthusiasm of his people, to everything that a popular leader loves. As he lay there on the ground alone before God, wishing himself back in Midian, and thinking himself hardly used, he was falling as a corn of wheat into the ground to die, no longer to abide alone, but to bear much fruit.

Ah, but dying is not pleasant work ! It is not easy nor pleasant to forgo one's own plans, to cease from one's own works, to renounce one's own reputation, to be despised and flouted by the very slaves you would save. What corn of wheat enjoys having its waterproof sheath torn from it, its elements disintegrated, its heart eaten into, as it lies helpless, exposed to the earth-forces, in the cold, damp, dark soil ? And yet this is the necessary condition which must be fulfilled, ere it can put forth the slender stalk, like a hand holding to the sun thirty, sixty, or a hundred grains like itself. "That which thou sowest is not quickened except it die; ... but if it die it bringeth forth much fruit."

It is a lesson for us all. God must bring us down before He can raise us up. Emptying must precede filling. We must get to an end of ourselves before He can begin in us. But what a beginning He makes ! "Then the Lord said unto Moses, Now thou shalt see what I will do to Pharaoh, for with a strong hand shall he let them go, and with a strong hand shall he drive them out of his land" (Exod. vi. 1). And as those words of encouragement and promise broke on his ear, he must have forgotten the averted looks and bitter words of the people, and risen into a new world of restful expectation. Deliverance was sure, though he had learned that it did not depend on anything that he could do, but on that all-sufficient God, who had announced Himself as the I AM.

And out of the whole story there comes to us this lesson: we must never suppose that the difficulties which confront us indicate that we are not on God's path, and doing his work. Indeed the contrary is generally the case. If we are willing to walk with God, He will test the sincerity and temper of our soul; He will cause men to ride over our heads; He will bring us through fire and through water. But out of all He will bring us into a large room, and give us the very thing on which we have been taught to set our hearts. The further banks of the Red Sea with their song of victory will wipe out the memory of those bitter disappointments, those sharp speeches, those hours of lonely anguish.

*

VIII

THE LOVE OF GOD IN THE FIRST FOUR PLAGUES

"Though the Lord cause grief, yet will He have compassion according
to the multitude of His mercies."
—LAM. iii. 32.

IN DESPAIR Moses had thrown himself on God, pouring out the story
of his failure and shame. "Wherefore hast Thou so evil entreated
this people ? why is it that Thou hast sent me ?" But there was no
chiding, no rebuke, on the part of his strong and faithful Friend, who
knew his frame, and remembered that he was but dust. "Then the
Lord said unto Moses, Now shalt thou see what I will do to
Pharaoh."

The emphasis lies on the words, *Then,—Now,—I. Then,*—when he
had reached the lowest point of self-confidence. *Now,*—since all
human effort has been put forth in vain. *I,*—the self-existent, ever-
glorious Lord. He will not give his glory to another. He is for our
sakes jealous of his honour. Therefore it is that He brings us down
to the dust of self-humiliation, empties us of human pride, divides
with his sharp two-edged sword between the energy of our soul-life
and the divine energy of His. Only when this is complete, and we
have drunk to the dregs the bitter cup of despair of self, does He
step in, saying in effect, "Child of my love, stand aside ; quiet thyself
as a weaned babe, and thou shalt see what I will do. I need thee not,
save as the vehicle and expression of the purpose which I have formed
in my heart, and which I am prepared to execute by my strong right
arm."

The time of depression with the discouraged servant of God is
always a time of promise. Then God takes to Himself a new name
(Exod. vi. 3) ; then He gives a glimpse of the meaning of his dealings
in the past (4) ; then He reveals the sympathy of his heart, which can
detect inarticulate groans (5) ; then, since He can swear by no other,
He pledges Himself with a sevenfold guarantee (6–8). Does any soul

cursed with the tyranny of a bondage beneath which all its energies are pressed to the dust peruse these lines? Let such an one lay to heart the repeated "I will" of this marvellous necklace of promises, which are Yea and Amen in Christ Jesus, applicable to all circumstances, parallel with all ages, unchangeable and eternal as the nature of Jehovah who gave them. "I will bring you out . . ., I will rid you . . ., I will redeem you . . ., I will take you to Me . . ., I will be to you a God . . ., I will bring you into the land . . ., I will give it you . . ."; and notice that this cluster of *I wills* is contained within two brackets, that pledge the very nature of God itself to their accomplishment, "I am the Lord (6) . . . I am the Lord" (8).

God always links obedience and promise. The doing his will must follow close upon the hearing his voice. Promise is intended as spur to action. We hear, that we may pass on to others the words that have stirred our spirits; and, therefore, it befell that Moses was recommissioned to speak, first to the children of Israel, and then to Pharaoh, king of Egypt. It must have been a very memorable day in which the summons came to him *in the land of Egypt*, as it had come before in the wilderness of Sinai (Exod. vi. 28).

Had it ever occurred to him that that vision and voice were inseparable from the solitude of those unfrequented wastes, and the silences of those everlasting hills; and that what was possible there, could have no counterpart amid the stir of Egyptian life, and the presence of the hoary monuments of idolatry? If so, the suggestion was at once answered by that voice finding him in Egypt itself. Ah! souls of men, God speaks not only in the stillness of the hermit's life; but amid the stir of active engagement, and the press of crowds.

It needed more than usual courage for the two brothers to undertake this further ministry; their people were too broken with anguish of spirit and disappointed hope to care very much what was said, especially when it was said by men who had been the cause of the increase of their burdens: and as for Pharaoh, it was idle to suppose that he would be touched by lips which had no power to charm the ears of Hebrews. "And Moses spake before the Lord, saying, Behold, the children of Israel have not hearkened unto me; how then shall Pharaoh hear me, who am of uncircumcised lips?" (chap. vi. 12). But it was not the time for parley. There was no doubt as to his duty, there should be no hesitation in his obedience.

At the outset of the interview, Pharaoh, as was expected, asked for their credentials, which they gave as God had instructed them. But the evidence was neutralized by the magicians counterfeiting them, either by the dexterity of their sleight-of-hand, or by collusion with that evil spirit, who has ever sought to mimic Divine work. It was significant, however, that Aaron's rod swallowed up their rods. But the great question would have to be settled on a wider arena, and by a series of more remarkable signs.

It is necessary that we should for a moment consider the underlying principle of God's dealings with Pharaoh, especially in the earlier plagues. And it will not be difficult to discern the operation of the eternal principles of Divine justice and love in the staggering blows which the Divine Power dealt to Pharaoh and his land.

I. THE LOVE OF GOD. Always and everywhere, God is Love. Whoso is wise with heavenly wisdom, and has eyes purged from the scales of prejudice and passion, will see as much of the tender mercy of God in the Old Testament as in the New; in the storm as in the zephyr; in the earthquake as in the still small voice; in the plagues as in the cross. The very term JEHOVAH, so constantly employed on these pages, indicates, first the unchangeableness, and then the redemptive side, of God's nature. And surely we must believe that Pharaoh was included in the love that gave Jesus Christ to the world; was embraced within the compass of his propitiation; and might have shone as a star in the firmament of blood-bought saints.

It must be possible, therefore, to find a clue which will reconcile the love of God, which brooded over Pharaoh and his land, with the apparent harshness that inflicted the successive plagues. And it will help us if we remember that there is a marked difference between the first four plagues and the rest. In the commencement of God's dealings with the tyrant it would almost appear as if He set Himself to answer the question, "Who is the Lord that I should obey his voice?" and to remove the ignorance of which he complained when he said, "I know not the Lord."

The case was this. Here was a man who from his earliest childhood had been accustomed to think that the deities of his nation were supreme in heaven and on earth; such as the bountiful goddess, who, from her secret urn, was ever pouring forth the waters of the sacred Nile, inundating the land with fertility and beauty; the prolific source of life, whose favourite emblem was the frog, which in unlimited numbers swarmed on the banks of the Nile ! whilst he would attach reverential importance to the purity of the priesthood, and the supremacy of the sun-god, of whom the beetle was the sacred sign. It would have been impossible to expect that in a single week he should turn away from these, to accept the commands of One whose name was, for the first time, uttered in his presence by the representatives of a nation of slaves.

When in Athens the Apostle Paul discovered an altar to THE UNKNOWN GOD. He did not rebuke the people for not having given Him suitable worship; but set himself to declare His nature and attributes. And he went on to show that nature, with all her marvellous processes, was due, not to the deities of the heathen Pantheon —though their effigies, sculptured by the art of Phidias, stood out before the gaze of his audience, irradiate with the pure light and unstained in the pure air—but was the creation of Him who had spoken to mankind in Jesus, and whose representative he was. And so God set Himself to show that the gods of the heathen were no gods; that the whole system of Egyptian worship must be subordinate to the empire of a greater God than any known to their magicians or priests; and that though He had winked at (to use the old expressive term) the days of past ignorance, the time had come when He commanded all men everywhere—Pharaoh on his throne, the priest in his temple, the ryot in his hut—to repent.

"Who is Jehovah?" He is the God of Nature, at whose bidding the Nile no longer blesses, but curses, her devotees; at whose command the objects of Egyptian worship become a loathing and an abomination, and make the land stink; at the expression of whose will the bodies of the priests are covered with the lice that deride all that razor or water can do for their extermination, and at whose summons the sacred beetle corrupts the land. "Not know Him?" He is the God who speaks through human voices; the God of the aged brethren; the God of those groaning serfs; the God who could not run back from a covenant into which He had entered with that long-suffering people; the God of Redemption and of Eternity.

II. THE FAITH OF MOSES.—Though it is quite true that the love of God was at work, seeking to reveal itself to Pharaoh by the ordering of the plagues; yet we must always remember that the faith of Moses played no inconspicuous part in respect to them. This is very apparent in connection with the last of the series, concerning which we are told "by faith he forsook Egypt"; and that "he endured, as seeing Him who is invisible." What was true, therefore, concerning the last, was probably true of the rest; and it becomes us to read into the story of Exodus the spiritual qualities unveiled to us in the Epistle to the Hebrews, where the Spirit of God draws aside the veil of the workings of his inner life and manifests him as he was.

In all probability, therefore, throughout the conflict which issued in the emancipation of Israel, Moses was closely dealing with God. God was vividly present to the eye of his soul. He thought much more of the presence and power of Jehovah than he did of the majesty and might of the greatest king of the time; and as God disclosed to him each successive stage of his providential dealings with Pharaoh, his faith claimed that He should do even as He had said. It was therefore through *his* faith, as the medium and instrument, that God wrought with his mighty hand and outstretched arm.

Are there any marvels recorded in Scripture which took place apart from the operation of the faith of some believing soul or souls ? If Enoch was translated as a warning to the antediluvian world, it was because he had faith for it. If Isaac was born to a mother who had renounced all hope of child-bearing, it was because her faith received strength. If the Red Sea yielded a path to the ransomed hosts, it was because their leader's faith rolled back the glassy billows. If the walls of Jericho fell down, it was because Joshua had faith to believe they would. Just as electricity must have a wire to conduct it, so the almighty power of God demands the organ of our faith. That faith may be very slender; the believer may be very deficient in what the world accounts most precious: but if only there be a genuine connection between the eternal God and the case that has to be met, it is enough. All the Godhead may pass through the slender faith of a very unworthy man; just as the ocean may pass through a very narrow channel. It is with such thoughts in our mind that we consider the first four plagues, and how God showed his love in them.

III. THE PLAGUES.—*The River.*—One morning, shortly after the events already described, as the sky would be covered with the roseate hue of dawn's first faint blush, Pharaoh, accompanied by high officials, court functionaries, and priests, came down either to perform his customary ablutions or to worship. Upon the river's brink he found Moses awaiting him, with the rod, with which he was already familiar, in his hand. There was no hesitation now in the peremptory summons, "The Lord God of the Hebrews hath sent me unto thee, saying, Let my people go, that they may serve Me in the wilderness." Then follow words which bear out what has been already said of God's purpose in the plagues, "In this shalt thou know that I am the Lord." The first revelation of God was to be made in the smitten water flowing blood; in the death of its fish, that formed not only objects of worship, but provided a large part of the food staple; and in the stench that filled the land with loathing.

The summons was met by the curled lip of scorn or imperturbable silence; and as there was no alternative, Aaron smote the water with the rod in the presence of the court. Most certainly, as he did so, the two brothers exercised faith that God would do as He had said; and according to their faith it befell. An instantaneous change passed over the appearance and the nature of the water. It became blood. From bank to brae, the tide of crimson gore swept on, hour after hour, day after day, till a week was fulfilled. The fish died, and floated on the surface. The air reeked with corruption. And the effects of the visitation extended throughout all the pools, and reservoirs, and cisterns, in places of public resort, as well as in the homes of the people. There was no water in all the land, save the scanty supplies obtained by digging shallow wells, and collecting the brackish surface water.

The magicians, in some way, counterfeited the marvel; and Pharaoh probably thought that on the part of Moses and Aaron there was only a superior sort of legerdemain. Therefore he did not set his heart to it, though he must have realized that he was at issue with a power greater than that of the goddess of the Nile.

Frogs.—It has been supposed that the plagues followed in rapid succession, so that the impression of one had not passed away before another succeeded it. And thus the whole conflict was probably comprehended within nine or ten months. It may have therefore been but a few days after, that Moses and Aaron renewed their demand for emancipation, and told the king the penalty of refusal. But there was no response, no proposal, and the inevitable blow fell.

The land suddenly swarmed with frogs. They came up from the river in myriads, till the very ground seemed alive with them, and it was impossible to walk far without crushing scores. Frogs in the houses, frogs in the beds, frogs baked with the food in the ovens, frogs in the kneading-troughs worked up with the flour; frogs with their monotonous croak, frogs with their cold, slimy skins, every-where—from morning to night, from night to morning—frogs. And the aggravation of the plague consisted in the fact of the frog being the emblem of the goddess of fecundity; so that it was sacrilege to destroy it.

This plague elicited from Pharaoh the first symptom of surrender. He sent for the brethren, and implored their prayers that the scourge might be removed, promising that compliance with his request would secure deliverance, "I will let the people go." To make the supremacy and power of God more manifest, Moses bade the monarch fix his own time for the staying of the plague, and then went to cry to the Lord: "Moses cried unto the Lord; and the Lord did according to the word of Moses."

It is remarkable that though the magicians counterfeited the coming of the frogs, they were evidently unable to remove them; and, indeed, the king does not appear to have appealed to them for help in this direction. Alleviation of human suffering is no part of the programme of the devil or his agents. That can only come from Jehovah, through the believing cry of his servants. But what a lesson was taught to Pharaoh—that Jehovah was above all gods, and that He alone could do according to his will!

Lice.—The Egyptians were scrupulously cleanly in their personal habits, anticipating the habits of our own time. And the priests were specially so. They bathed themselves repeatedly, and constantly shaved their persons, that no uncleanliness might unfit them for their sacred duties. What horror, then, must have taken hold of them when the very dust of Egypt seemed breeding lice; and they found that they were not exempted from the plague, which was as painful as it was abhorrent to their delicate sensibility.

Perhaps there is something more than appears at first sight in the words, "there was lice in man and *in beast*." Not only on the bodies of the priests, but on those of the sacred beasts, was there this odious pest. Each revered shrine boasted its sacred bull or goat, whose glossy skin was cleansed with reverent care; and it was an unheard-of calamity that it should become infested with this most disgusting parasite. Thus upon the gods of Egypt did God execute judgment, in order that Pharaoh might know that He was God of gods, deserving of the allegiance which He claimed. The magicians themselves seem to have felt that this plague was a symptom of the working of a higher Power than they knew; and even they urged Pharaoh to consider that it was the finger of God. How often do unexpected voices read for us the lessons that God designs to teach!

The Beetle.—It is not perfectly certain what is meant by the word translated "flies." And though it is possible that it is rightly rendered "flies," yet it is quite as likely that it stands for a peculiar kind of beetle, which was the emblem of the sun-god. Their most powerful deity seemed now to have turned against them, and to have become their scourge at the behest of the God of these shepherd-slaves. The beetles covered the ground, swarmed into the houses, and spoilt the produce of their land.

That it was no mere natural visitation was made clear by a division being made in this plague between the land of Egypt and that of Goshen, where the Israelites were found. This God, who could turn the very deities of Egypt against their votaries, could as evidently protect his own. And perhaps this wrought on Pharaoh's heart, as nothing else had done; for he was prepared to allow the Israelites to sacrifice in the land. It was a concession which Moses could not accept; alleging that the Israelites would be obliged to sacrifice as victims animals which the Egyptians considered sacred, and irritated feeling might provoke some terrible outbreak of violence. Pharaoh yielded to this reason; and promised to let them go, if they did not go very far, on the condition, that Moses should secure the removal of the plague. "And the Lord did according to the word of Moses."

In all this Moses was but the medium, the ambassador, the instrument through whom God wrought. The suggestion of the plagues lay with the Almighty; their execution was effected through the strong faith of the faithful servant, who did as he was told, and spoke as he was bidden. And it was in answer to his believing prayer that the plagues ceased. Through faith like that God will pass out to do his work of might and love and salvation amongst men.

IX

How the Character of Moses Grew

"Moses was faithful in all his house."
—Heb. iii. 2.

If we were engaged in telling the story of the Exodus, it would become us to study minutely the account of the succeeding plagues. But the story of Israel is, for our present purpose, incidental to the study of that great personage who gave tone and character to the mighty movement which issued in the passage of the Red Sea. It is on Moses that our attention must be focused; and, indeed, it is marvellous to trace the growth of this man, in perhaps a few months, from the diffidence and hesitancy of Midian to the moral sublimity which made him "very great in the land of Egypt," in the sight of the great officials of the court, no less than of the mass of the common people (Gen. xi. 3).

We can trace this development of character through the remaining plagues; and as we do so we shall inevitably discover that the secrets of growth consist in an instant and unquestioning obedience, an utter indifference to human opinion, strength of purpose, unfailing patience, indomitable courage, persevering faith and prayer.

Murrain.—In the earlier part of his ministry Moses had repeatedly questioned with God before he set about the performance of the Divine commissions. "Who am I, that I should go in unto Pharaoh ?" "How shall Pharaoh hear me who am of uncircumcised lips ?" "Behold, I am of uncircumcised lips; how shall Pharaoh hearken unto me ?" And, using the language of men, it needed much persuasion and entreaty before he would fulfil Jehovah's word.

But all that had vanished now. Though he had been at least seven times in the royal presence, and each time the bearer of heavy tidings, increasingly abhorred by Pharaoh and his court, and though so far his appearances there had been unsuccessful in securing the great object which God had set before him, yet there was no hesitancy or questioning, when for the eighth time the Lord bade him present himself in the palace to demand the emancipation of the people on pain of a murrain on the beasts.

It is hardly possible to over-estimate the value of simple, unquestioning obedience in the growth of character. The rejection of Saul, the first king of Israel, and the selection of David hinged on the fact that the one did not obey the voice of the Lord in performing his commandments, and that the other was a man after God's heart and fulfilled all his will. The stress of our Lord's farewell discourse is on the reiterated word *obey*. Obedience is the test of love; the condition of divine revelation; the precursor of the most sacred intimacy into which God can enter with the human spirit. In proportion as we obey, we become possessed of noble elements of character; which exist in our hearts as vapour until they are condensed in some act of obedience, and become henceforth a permanent property. Disbelief and disobedience are interchangeable terms (Heb. iv. 11, marg.); from which we may infer that as our obedience is, so will our faith become. Live up to what you know to be your duty; fill in the outlines of God's commands; never stay to count consequences or to question results; if God says, "Go unto Pharaoh and tell him," and you obey, you will not only be set to greater tasks, but you will acquire a character which no amount of meditation or prayer could afford.

The murrain came at the fixed time, "and the cattle of Egypt died." The cattle that fed on the green meadows of the Nile; the horses of the wealthy, for which Egypt was famous; the asses of the poor; the camels that bore the merchandise of Egypt afar, in exchange for spices and balm and myrrh (Gen. xxxvii. 25); the oxen that ploughed the fields; the sheep which constituted so large a proportion of their wealth—on all of these the murrain fell. The land was filled with death; the rich land-owners were greatly impoverished; the poor suffered severely; thousands of shepherds and teamsters were thrown out of work; the routine of business communication was seriously interrupted; and evidence was given of the increasing severity of the plague: whilst God's care for his own was clearly shown in the cordon of protection that He placed around Goshen, concerning which it is said, "Of the cattle of the children of Israel died not one."

Boils and Blains.—In estimating a man's work we must always consider the character of the man himself. Certain kinds of work, congenial to some dispositions, are most distasteful to others; and you might as well look for apples on vines as expect to find the two in conjunction. It is much more startling to find certain attributes in some characters than in others—it is like finding a layer of gneiss in chalk. And, surely, it must have been a much greater effort for Moses to be the medium of such judgments, and the object of so much bitter hatred, than for many. He was naturally gentle, tender, and very meek—always ready to pray for the cessation of a plague, and never for its advent; yearning sympathetically over sister and brother, though they had grievously injured him; willing to be accursed if the people might be spared. A man who had kept sheep for forty years would be likely to acquire a tender shepherd-heart. And it must have been no small effort to be the instrument for inflicting pain. Yet this fell plentifully to his lot in his terrible vindication of the supremacy and sovereignty of God.

But he flinched not. It was not for him to aspire to be more pitiful than God; and, therefore, when Aaron and he were bidden to take ashes from some expiring furnace, and fling them broadcast on the air, to become a boil breaking forth with blains upon man and upon beast, he did not hesitate. Taking in his hands handfuls of ashes, he accosted Pharaoh on some public occasion, when he and his court of magicians were assembled in the open air, and sprinkled the light grey dust up towards heaven; with such immediate effect that "the magicians could not stand before him because of the boils, for the boil was upon the magicians and upon all Egyptians" (ver. 11), and, perhaps, penetrated also to the sacred precincts of the temples, breaking out in the beasts which were there zealously kept free from taint, as gods of the nation (Num. xxxiii. 4).

The Hail.—As the plagues advance, Aaron is increasingly dropped out of sight. In the first three plagues the Lord said distinctly unto Moses, "Say unto Aaron" (vii. 19; viii. 5, 16). In the fourth (viii. 20) and fifth (ix. 1), the word was to Moses only. In the sixth the command is to them both (ix. 8). But in this, the seventh, the command is given exclusively to Moses. "The Lord said unto Moses, Stretch forth thine hand toward heaven, that there may be hail" (ver. 22). And so with the plagues of locusts (x. 12), and of the darkness that might be felt (x. 21). Why this was we are not told. It does not appear that Aaron had in any way forfeited his position by misconduct; but he may have lacked that simplicity and directness and purity of motive which were so characteristic of his brother: and the faith of Moses grew with every trial of the faithfulness and reliableness of God, till it alone was able to act as the vehicle of the Divine Will. In any case, Moses came increasingly to the front as the wielder of the miracle-working rod, and as the emancipator of Israel.

In the present instance, also, he seems to have acquired to a surprising extent the power of speech. Those stammering lips became the channels of unwonted eloquence, and were kindled by unexpected fire. It was as if he had suddenly felt able to lay aside the mediation of Aaron, and to claim those words which the Almighty had promised to put into his mouth. And is it not full of comfort to find that the Lord did not keep him to the mistaken bargain he had made, that Aaron should be his spokesman (Exod. iv. 15–17). We may have said rash things in the past, which we now deeply and seriously regret; but if we show ourselves worthy of a greater destiny than our weak faith imagined possible, God may not tie us to our words, but will open before us possibilities of which we had not dreamt. Aaron shall not be our mouth-piece; we will stand and speak for ourselves.

The warning given to Pharaoh in that early morning was a very solemn one; but it was in vain. He had deliberately hardened himself so often that now both warning and appeal fell on him like rain and sun on granite slabs, and even tended to harden his heart still more. There is no ice so hard as that which melts by day and freezes by night.

And so the storm broke. As the rod was uplifted, vast thunder-clouds drifted up from the sea, and covered the land, and poured out their contents in thunder, hail, and fire. Storms of any kind are very rare in Egypt; and this was "very grevious, such as there was none like it in all the land of Egypt since it became a nation." There are several references in the Psalms to this fearful visitation. We can almost hear the peal of the thunder, and detect the devastation caused by the hail, in the vibrating chords of Hebrew minstrelsy. In the intervals of the thunder-peals, in which the Almighty uttered his voice, we can hear the pelt of the hailstone chorus and the explosion of the balls of fire (Psa. xviii. 12, 13). The vines torn from their trellises and beaten into the soil; the sycamore trees blighted as by frost; the forest-trees broken down; the crops of flax and barley utterly spoilt; beasts and herdsmen unsheltered in the open fields in defiance of the warning given, smitten to death by hailstones, which fell as thick as rain, and may have weighed (as in exceptional instances hailstones have been known to weigh) from six to eight ounces—such are some of the indications given of the terror of the scene (Psa. lxxviii. 47, 48; cv. 32). But from all these the land of Goshen was free.

Through the pelting storm, Moses and Aaron were summoned into the royal presence to hear for the first time from those proud lips the confession of sin (Exod. ix. 27); with an urgent entreaty that the mighty thunderings and hail which were then shaking palace and city might cease. Moses had no doubt as to the answer which would come to his prayer; but he had grave doubts of the reliableness of the royal word. However, he did as Pharaoh required. Passing uninjured through the storm, he went beyond the city gates into the open country. It was as if he consciously lived in the secret place of the Most High, and abode under the shadow of the Almighty. With outspread hands he interceded for the land of the oppressors of his people; and God hearkened to his request: so that the thunders and hail ceased, and the rain was no more poured out upon the earth (ver. 33).

The Locusts.—The tone of Moses rose with every plague. Hitherto he had been content with repeating his demand; but now the failure of the king to keep his royal word had altered the relations between them. Pharaoh had forfeited all claim to his respect. He had made repeated promises and broken them. His confessions of sin had been followed by no efforts at amendment. He was no longer ignorant of Jehovah, but wilfully obstinate and defiant. Weak, vacillating, cringing in trial, imperious and truculent in prosperity, he had become unspeakably despicable. And Moses altered his tone; not now treating him as a sovereign, but as a sinner, and dealing directly with his proud and obstinate heart: "Thus saith the Lord God of the Hebrews, How long wilt thou refuse to humble thyself before Me?" The penalty of further delay was to be an infliction of locusts.

The Egyptians well knew what a plague of locusts might mean; and therefore the servants of Pharaoh pleaded with the king to acquiesce in the demand of the Hebrew leaders. Better lose a nation of slaves, said they, than imperil the land. So that from that moment it became a trial of strength between the king of Egypt and God, in whom for the first time in his history he had found more than his match.

Pharaoh, at his servants' suggestion, proposed a compromise. He was willing to let *the men* go, and threatened them with evil if they did not accept this proposition. But there was no hesitation in its instant refusal by the brothers. It could not be. The young and old must go, sons and daughters, flocks and herds—*all.* None was to be absent in that great convocation, which was to assemble somewhere in the desert to hold a feast to Jehovah. The court had never heard the great Pharaoh so addressed; nor could he endure that dauntless speech; so, at a signal from him, they were driven from his presence.

But the locusts came with an east wind, which, blowing straight from the desert, had set in on the land for a whole day and night. "When it was morning, the east wind brought the locusts." Their numbers filled the air, and literally covered the earth. Its green surface was darkened by their brown forms; and every trace of green in the fields, on the fruit trees, and among the plentiful herbs, of which the Egyptians were so fond, instantly disappeared. There was no bud, nor blossom, nor shoot, nor leaf, left anywhere "through all the land of Egypt" (x. 15). The animals had perished, and now the produce of the earth. Surely the next visitation must sweep away all human life. Panic-stricken, the king sent for the men whom a little before he had driven from his presence; confessed that he had not only sinned against Jehovah, who had now become an evident Personality to his conscience, but against them; and entreated that this death might be removed. How gracious and long-suffering is God ! In answer to Moses' intercession, "the Lord turned a mighty strong west wind, which took away the locusts, and cast them into the Red Sea; there remained not one locust in all the coasts of Egypt" (ver. 19). But again Pharaoh went back from his word.

The Darkness.—Unannounced, the darkness fell like a pall upon the land, "even darkness that could be felt." Travellers tell us of darkness caused by sand-storm, so thick that it was impossible to see the hand when placed close against the face. From whatever cause, the darkness of this plague must have been of the same description.

"They saw not one another, neither rose any from his place for three days." All the activities of the land were paralysed. The stoutest hearts were dismayed. It seemed as if their greatest deity had suddenly deserted them, abandoning their case. Perhaps the light would never visit them again. In that land of radiant sunlight it was an awful experience. The very temples were so draped in gloom that the priests could not see the sacred beasts, nor were they able to perform their usual rites. For the first time in perhaps centuries great Memnon's statue failed to greet the beams of the morning sun with music.

When the plague passed away, for the last time the monarch summoned the brothers, and made a final desperate effort at compromise. The nation might go, said he; but the flocks and herds must remain. But Moses penetrated the craft of the proposal, and tore it to shreds. "Our cattle shall go with us, there shall not an hoof be left behind." Clearly they would be required for sacrifice (ver. 25). Then, again, the proud spirit of the king, uncowed by repeated misfortune, untaught by the stern discipline of pain, broke vehemently forth; and he said, as if exasperated beyond endurance, "Get thee from me, take heed to thyself, see my face no more; for in that day thou seest my face thou shalt die" (ver. 28).

The spirit of Moses, also, was swept with that anger which at rare intervals asserted itself in him, as a storm on a tranquil lake (Exod. xi. 8); but he made answer with calm dignity, as became the ambassador of God. "And Moses said, Thou hast spoken well; I will see thy face again no more" (ver. 29). But as he turned to leave the royal presence, he raised himself to his full height, and poured one overwhelming torrent of denunciation and warning on the wilful spirit that had deliberately chosen evil for its god, and destruction for its doom. "And Moses said, Thus saith the Lord, About midnight will I go out into the midst of Egypt; and all the firstborn of Egypt shall die. And all these thy servants shall come down unto me, and bow down themselves unto me, saying, Get thee out, and all the people that follow thee; and after that I will go out" (xi. 4–8).

Thus did the bowing reed of Midian become as a rock on which the tempest expends its force in vain; the man who had left that palace in fear, strode its courts as a king; and the faith which fled before the serpent-rod became strong enough to wield the thunderbolts of heaven, and to bring the land of Egypt to the very brink of destruction.

X

Preparing for the Exodus

"And it came to pass at the end of the four hundred and thirty years, . . . that all the hosts of the Lord went out from the land of Egypt."

—Exod. xii. 41.

WE HAVE seen how, during those months of agony, Moses had been the organ through which God wrought out his purposes; first of informing Pharaoh's mind, and latterly of breaking his stubborn will. And already we have had indications that through the faith of this man, which was growing exceedingly, blessing would accrue to the chosen people.

The first three plagues fell equally on the children of Israel as on the Egyptians; but when the brothers threatened Pharaoh with the fourth, they were commissioned, in the name of God, to utter this further message: "I will sever in that day the land of Goshen, in which my people dwell" (Exod. viii. 22). And from that hour the children of Israel were exempted from the terrible inflictions by which Egypt was desolated. Moses claimed that God should do as He had said. And according to his faith it befell. No murrain swept off their beasts. No boils broke out on their persons. No tempest swept their fields. No locusts destroyed their crops. No darkness obscured to them the sun. Thus, while the minds of their oppressors were engrossed with their own special sufferings, the Hebrews were at peace; and when the Egyptians were prevented by the darkness from moving, the oppressed population of Goshen had ample time to prepare for that Exodus which Moses at least knew was so near.

As we study that strange and marvellous episode, we must never forget the light thrown on it by the memorable verse which tells us that "*by faith* Moses kept the Passover, and the sprinkling of blood; lest he that destroyed the first-born should touch them" (Heb. xi. 28). The importance of this verse lies in the fact that it attributes the keeping of the Passover, the sprinkling of blood on the lintels of the

Hebrew houses, and the immunity of the Hebrew people, to the effect of the heroic faith which burnt so steadily in the soul of this simple-hearted man; the entirety of whose obedience was only equalled by the absoluteness of the unquestioning faith, which dared to take God at his word.

I. His Faith was Based on Promise.—All faith must rest there. There must be some distinct word or undertaking on the part of one who is perfectly trustworthy, or there is no ground for faith to build on. Here is the difference between faith and credulity; between faith and following some vain will-o'-the-wisp, generated amid the miasma of an unhealthy imagination.

We cannot tell the form in which the Divine Word came to the two brethren. Was it as when a man speaketh to his friend? Should we have heard it, with our uncircumcised ears, had we been in their company? Or was it an impression photographed on the heart of each, upturned towards the source of light? But, howsoever the communication came, in those accents—which first declared what Israel was to do, and then, with unhesitating precision, announced the successive acts which would finally smite the fetters from the captives' hands, and free the nation in a single night—they recognised the voice that had bidden them go to Pharaoh with repeated summonses to surrender.

The directions were substantially these. On the tenth of the following month, the head of each family, whether slave or elder, was to select a firstling lamb, free of disease and defect. Only if the family were too small to need a lamb for itself might it join with some neighbouring household. There was no question as to the lamb being too little for the household. Jesus is "enough for all, enough for each, enough for ever more." The lamb was to be kept from the tenth to the fourteenth of the month, and killed on the latter day, towards the close of the afternoon. The blood, as it gushed warm from the wound, was to be carefully caught in a basin, and sprinkled on the two side posts and lintel of the houses where the Israelites dwelt; the carcase roasted whole, and eaten with unleavened bread and bitter herbs.

Special instructions were also given as to the attitude in which that feast was to be eaten. The whole family was to be gathered around the table, from the grey-headed sire to the new-born babe. There was to be no symptom of lassitude or indolence. The men were to have their loins girt as for a long journey, and to grasp their staves. The women were to have their dough and kneading troughs bound up in little bundles, with their clothes, for easy carriage on their shoulders. All were to have their feet sandalled. The meal was to be eaten in haste. And thus, with ears intent to catch the first note of the trumpet, the whole nation was to await the signal for its Exodus, sheltered by blood; whilst strength was stored for the fatigues that must be endured ere the land of bondage was left behind for ever.

There was a great contrast, therefore, between the attitude of the Israelites in the destruction of the first-born and in the former plagues. In those they had been perfectly inactive, only reaping the benefits which accrued from the successive victories won through the faith of their great leader. But now they were called upon to appropriate benefits, which might not accrue if they failed to conform to the conditions laid down. And in those demands on their obedience and faith, there surely must have broken, on the minds of the more intelligent at least, the feeling that there was a deeper meaning in the whole transaction than appeared on the surface; and that eternal issues were being wrought out, the meaning of which they could not as yet adequately apprehend.

Moses at least must have felt that God was in effect saying to his people that they were not less guilty, in some respects, than the Egyptians around them. It was not enough for them to allege that they had not gone to the same lengths of stiff-necked rebellion as Pharaoh and his people. Had they not forgotten his Sabbaths, and turned to serve other gods, and mingled in the evil rites of Egyptian idolatry? For these things, at least, they were held guilty in his sight, and liable to lose the first-born of their homes, unless they kept the sprinkling of blood.

And when all the provisions had been thus solemnly recited, there followed the words of promise, on which thenceforward Moses reposed his faith; "I will pass through the land of Egypt, and will smite all the first-born in the land of Egypt, both man and beast; ... and when I see the blood, I will pass over you, and the plague shall not be upon you to destroy you, when I smite the land of Egypt" (ver. 12, 13).

II. HIS FAITH LED TO ACTION.—He gathered the elders of Israel, and informed them of the instructions he had received; and whether it was that some prognostications of their coming deliverance had entered their souls, or that they had come to believe in their great leader to an extent which had been previously impossible, it is certain that they offered neither opposition nor suggestion to his proposals. They bowed the head and worshipped, and went their way to do "as the Lord had commanded Moses and Aaron: so did they" (ver. 27, 28).

It is a glorious thing for men and angels to see a faith which, with no outward appearance to warrant it, will yet step out on a path of literal obedience, though there seems nothing but thin air to tread upon. It seemed so utterly extraordinary for such a thing to be, as the deliverance of his people, because blood happened to be sprinkled on the outside of their doors. There was no precedent; no apparent reason to justify such a thing to ordinary common-sense; no likelihood of obedience having any connection with deliverance. Many such thoughts may have occurred to him; but he dismissed them from his mind, and simply obeyed, believing that there could be no mistake, no shadow of turning in Him to whom he had given the allegiance of his soul.

Oh that such faith were ours ! Not arguing, nor questioning, nor reasoning: but believing that the promises of God are Yea and Amen in Christ; and that what He says about accepting all who believe in Christ, making us sit together with Him on his throne, and loving us with the love He bears his Son, He is willing and able to perform.

And such faith becomes contagious. How did that memorable tenth night of the month Abib close in upon Egypt ? Did not the air seem oppressed with the burden of the coming woe ? Did no priestess, intoxicated with Mephitic vapour, utter in piercing shrieks some warning of the terrible visitation at hand ? Did not the wings of the Angel of Death overshadow the doomed land, before he smote with his sword ? Surely the fact of the Israelites obtaining so many gifts of jewellery and raiment from the Egyptians indicated that, on both sides, there was an anticipation of their near release. Whilst, however, on the one hand, there must have been grave foreboding and suspense; on the other there were expectancy and hope. The faith of Moses had kindled faith in three millions of people; who stood ready to plunge the knife into the fleecy victim that awaited it, to sprinkle the blood, to start on the distant march, but with no fear that the first-born of the house should be left a corpse behind. No father eyed his son with anxiety; no mother trembled to hear the rustle of the angel-wing; no boy shuddered at the near approach of death. It was enough that God had said, that, when He saw the blood, He would pass over. But though they could not see it or understand it, or fathom the purposes of God, they knew the blood was there to speak for them; and they believed, therefore, that all must be well. And though no one knew exactly their destination, nor how they would reach it, they had no misgiving as to the issue.

III. HIS FAITH WAS VINDICATED.—Who can depict that night, ever memorable in the history of our race—when, indeed, as Bunsen says, history itself was born—the night when God brought Israel out of the house of bondage! It was the early spring, and a time of the full silver moon, which shed her soft light in cascades of beauty on the land that lay beneath her; from where, on the Western frontier, the Nile rolled its majestic volumes, to the waters of the Red Sea on the far Eastern border. All was still with an almost preternatural silence; "broken only by the hoot of the owl, the scream of the bittern, the plunge of the monster in the water, or the cry of the jackal on the plains."

But suddenly the stillness was interrupted by a scream of anguish, as a mother rushed out into the night to tell that the Angel of Death had begun his work, and she was presently answered by the wail of a mother in agony for her first-born; and this by another, and yet another. It was useless to summon priest or physician, magician or courtier; how could they help others who had not been able to ward off death from their own? The maid grinding at the mill and her lady sleeping under curtains of silk were involved in a common sorrow, which obliterated all social distinctions, and made all one. There was not a house where there was not one dead—even Pharaoh's palace was not exempt. The news spread like wildfire that the heir to the throne was dead. "And there was a great cry in Egypt."

Ah, Egypt! bitter as that night was, it did not counterbalance the wrongs that Israel had suffered at thy hands for centuries! Thy tears were as a rill, compared to the rivers of sorrow which had been extorted from that high-spirited people, who were compelled to turn the soil to brick, with no reward but the task-master's scourge! Thy loss in sweet and noble life was insignificant, compared with the thousands flung into the Nile, or done to death in the cruel brick-kilns! Thy cry, piercing and heartrending though it were, a whisper, compared with the sobs wrung from mothers as their babes were torn from their breasts, the groans of the oppressed as they saw their dear ones failing under a bondage they could not alleviate, or with the cries of the men driven to despair.

"Then Pharaoh rose up in the night, he and all his servants, and all the Egyptians; and he called for Moses and Aaron by night, and said, 'Rise up, and get you forth from among my people.'" There was no attempt at parley. They, their people, their children, and their property, were to be gone. And the bidding of the palace was repeated by ten thousand tongues. The one eager desire of the Egyptians was to get rid of them at all speed, and at all cost. They were glad to give them anything they asked, and thus bestowed some payment for their long unremunerated labour; and even Pharaoh, the haughty monarch, entreated that they would bless him ere they went.

And so the host stepped forth into freedom. For the first time the Israelites realized that they were a nation, and drank the earliest rich deep draught of liberty. A mere horde of slaves, they suddenly crystallized into a people. The spirit of their leader inspired and thrilled them. There was a fire in their eye, an elasticity in their step, a courage in their heart, which told their own story. Then was their mouth filled with laughter, and their tongue with singing. God hath made bare his holy arm in their deliverance. And sentiments began to assert themselves which were destined ere long to roll in thunderous acclaim along the shores of the Red Sea. What faith did for them it will do for thee and me, O soul enslaved by a worse tyranny than Pharaoh's. If only thou wouldst claim deliverance thou shouldst have it. Listen to the song which heralded the work of Christ: "that we, being delivered out of the hand of our enemies, might serve Him without fear, in holiness and righteousness all our days" (Luke i. 74, 75). This is for us. We, too, may overcome by the blood of the Lamb, and by the word of our testimony. By faith we, too, may obtain promises and stop the mouths of lions, and quench the violence of fire. Only claim thy freedom, and thou shalt tread on the lion and adder; the young lion and dragon shalt thou trample under foot.

XI

The Passage of the Red Sea

"The waters were a wall unto them on their right hand, and on their left. Thus the Lord saved Israel out of the hand of the Egyptians."
—Exod. xiv. 29, 30.

It was not long after the hour of midnight before the entire Israelite host was on the move; and as the morning light suffused the cloudlets with its flush, it beheld them marching, the men five abreast, whilst wives and children and baggage and cattle followed. From different points the vast host—which, judging by the fact that the number of the men amounted to six hundred thousand, could not have been less than two and a half millions—converged towards the central meeting-place at Succoth.

Moses probably led the largest of several detachments; and we can almost imagine the flush of honest pride upon his face, mingling with a sense of profound humility, that he had been honoured, in the hand of God, to become the instrument of so great a deliverance.

Succoth would be about fifteen miles from their starting-place, and there they made their first prolonged halt; baked unleavened cakes of the dough which they had brought with them; rested the weary women and children in leafy tabernacles hastily improvised from the foliage of that region: so that the whole host, heartened and refreshed, was able to undertake its second stage, which was Etham, on the edge of the wilderness, where the green vegetation of Egypt fades into wastes of sand. There is one episode in this setting forth that we must not forget to mention, and which shows how largely the whole Exodus was wrought in faith, at least in the case of Moses, and perhaps of more. "And Moses took the bones of Joseph with him" (xiii. 19). This great ancestor of their race had been dead some four hundred years; but on his death-bed he had made his brethren swear that when God visited them, as He most surely would, and brought them out of Egypt, they should bear his bones with them in their march. In his death, and through that weary waiting time, he had been the prophet of the Exodus; and how often must those unburied bones have been the theme of conversation in Hebrew homes ! And now that they were accompanying their march, all the people realized that the anticipations of generations were being fulfilled. "God had surely visited them."

I. THE GUIDING PILLAR.—In the campaigns of Alexander the Great, we are told that a brazier filled with combustibles and elevated on a high pole indicated his pavilion, and directed the march of his victorious armies. But a still greater spectacle came into view as that Hebrew host broke away from the land of bondage. Who has not seen in a summer sky some majestic cumulus cloud sailing slowly through the heavens, as if it had taken the impression of some mighty Alp, whose cliffs, recesses and snows were being reduplicated in its shape and colour? Something of this sort must have gathered in the pure morning atmosphere at the head of the vanguard, never again to desert that pilgrim band till the Jordan was crossed and it had settled down to brood over the house of God. But all through the years, when night fell, it burnt with fire at its heart; fire, which was always the symbol and sign of the presence of God.

This served many purposes. It was the guide of their march; it was a shadow from the burning heat of a vertical sun, spreading its folds in fleecy beauty to shelter them in a "weary land"; and at night it provided them with a light as it watched over them like the Eye of God. On one occasion, at least, as we shall see presently, it rendered the utmost service by concealing the movements of Israel, lying between them and the pursuit of their foes.

There is no pillar of cloud and fire now—long since it has faded from the sky; but it was in probable allusion to its blessed help that Jesus said, "I am the Light of the World," indicating by his use of a well-known phrase, that what the cloud had been to Israel, He was prepared to be to every soul of man.

He is our Guide; by his Spirit within us, by the example of his life, by the words of his Gospel, and by the manifold indications of his providence, He conducts us over the wastes of our earthly pilgrimage to the land where we would fain be. Do not anticipate Him by rash haste, or by acting on your own hurriedly-formed conclusions. Do not lag behind Him indolently. Dare to wait for months, or even years, if He give no indication that the time has come to strike your tents and follow.

He is our Shield; beneath his canopy we may shelter from the arrows of the sun of temptation or of prosperity, and from the glare of worldly success.

He is our light; those who follow Him do not walk in the darkness of ignorance, impurity, or sorrow, but have the light of life. Draw the curtain of your tent, Christian pilgrim ! look out into the night already glowing with the myriad stars of promise; amid them all behold the sign that *He* is with you, who slumbers not, nor sleeps, and to whom the night shineth as the day.

In the thought of Moses, that cloud by day and night must have been full of reassurance, because it was the very chariot of God, in which He went before his people. And it is very touching to learn that "He took it not away," as if neither sin, nor murmuring, nor disobedience, could ever drive away Him who loves us, not because we are good, but to make us so; and who cannot leave or forsake those whom He has taught to lisp, "Abba, Father."

II. THE ROUTE.—The easiest route to Canaan lay through the Isthmus of Suez and the land of the Philistines. A journey of a little over one hundred miles would have conducted them direct to their destination. But God did not permit them to go that way, lest the sight of embattled hosts should unnerve them. In after years, when the education and revelations of the desert were finished, they might behold those scenes undismayed. But as yet they must not know war till they had been more deeply taught in the might and care of God. So is our journey ever adapted to our strength. God is always considering what we are able to bear; never leading us into dangers before which heart and flesh would succumb. "God led them about." The leading about tries our patience; but it is the best route for timid hearts and inexperienced feet.

It must have been a great disappointment when the cloud altered its course, and led them due south. But there was no alternative; and so they finally found themselves encamped in the last place in all the land that human judgment would have selected. It would appear as if Moses himself would have hesitated encamping there, had he not been distinctly commanded to bid the children of Israel take up that position. On one side of them was Migdol (the modern Muktala) and impassable wastes of sand; on the other was the Red Sea. East of them, or, as it might be, in front, was the impassable range of Baal-Zephon.

It was a perfect *cul-de-sac*. There was no egress from it except the way by which they had entered. The most inexperienced eyes in the whole multitude must have seen the apparent absurdity of the movement; and loud and deep must have been the murmurs and protestations of the people. "Is this the way to Canaan? We know better! How dare you presume to lead us, when your very first tactics prove you to be wholly untrustworthy? Well for you and us that Pharaoh has his son to bury; or if he came after us we should be like a penned flock of sheep, the prey of the first wolf that can leap the hurdles!"

Such reflections and reproaches are not easy to bear. They can only be borne by a man who has learnt utterly to trust his God. But they made no impression on Moses. He knew Him whom he believed. He had learnt to obey Him implicitly, and to see himself always completely vindicated. "Though a host should encamp against him, his heart should not fear; though war should rise against him, in this would he be confident." Oh for more of this simple trust in God, which rests so distinctly in his guidance and help!— that the believer will dare to do what to the eye of others are marks of insanity and wild fanaticism, but which are vindicated by the result.

Often God seems to place his children in positions of profound difficulty—leading them into a wedge from which there is no escape; contriving a situation which no human judgment would have permitted had it been previously consulted. The very cloud conducts them thither. You, reader, may be thus involved at this very hour. It does seem perplexing and mysterious to the last degree. But it is perfectly right. The issue will more than justify Him who has brought you hither. It is a platform for the display of his almighty grace and power. He will not only deliver you, but in doing so He will give you a lesson that you will never forget; and to which, in many a psalm and song in after days, you will revert. You will never be able to thank God enough for having done just as He has. Had you brought yourself into this position by your caprice, you had perished miserably; but since He has brought you here, you have only to stand still and see his salvation, which is prepared as the morning.

III. THE PURSUIT.—No sooner had Israel gone than Pharaoh was sorry. The public works stood still for lack of labour. Vast territories were suddenly unoccupied. The labour of this enslaved people was missed on every side, in city and field. There was a sudden loss of revenue and service which he could ill dispense with. And his pride forbade that he should quietly acquiesce in their unhindered Exodus. Besides, in their mad haste to be rid of this people, the Egyptians had laden them with jewels of silver, and jewels of gold, and raiment; so much so that it is distinctly said, "they spoiled the Egyptians." It is clear from the contributions afterwards made to the building of the Tabernacle, that Israel was carrying off a large amount of treasure and valuables. "And the heart of Pharaoh, and of his servants, was turned against the people; and they said, Why have we done this, that we have let Israel go from serving us?" (xiv. 5, 6).

At this juncture, the king heard of the extraordinary movement southwards, which seemed to have thrown them again into his power. Surely his gods were recovering their olden power, and were rallying to his aid! And he said, "I will pursue; I will overtake; I will divide the spoil; my lust shall be satisfied upon them!" Then there was great haste, and the marshalling of the chivalry and the pride of Egypt, six hundred of the chosen chariots, with cavalry and infantry, horsemen and foot-soldiers. "And the Egyptians pursued after them, all the horses and chariots of Pharaoh . . . and overtook them" (xiv. 9).

And so as the afternoon closed in, of perhaps the fifth day of the Exodus, the outposts of the fugitive host beheld the dreaded forms of the Egyptian warriors coming over the ridges of the desert hills; and as the night fell they were aware that the whole Egyptian host was encamped in their near vicinity, only waiting for the morning light to swoop down on them, involving them either in a general massacre, or in what was, perhaps, more dreadful, a return to slavery.

It was an awful plight. Terrible, indeed, was the breaking of that news on those craven hearts. They immediately turned on Moses, and spent their fear and anguish on his heart. "Wherefore hast thou dealt thus with us? Were there no graves in Egypt? Better to have perished there than here ! Why did you not leave us alone ? Where is your God ?" And then that noble spirit rose up in the might of its faith, and in the words he spake we read his own inner attitude. He was not fearful nor dismayed, his cheeks were unblanched, his heart untroubled; he was standing still to see God's salvation, he was perfectly sure that it would be forthcoming that day; and he knew that Jehovah would fight for them, and redeem them, and vindicate his word. So we shall see in our next chapter.

XII

THE SONG OF VICTORY

"Sing ye to the Lord, for he hath triumphed gloriously; the horse and
his rider hath He thrown into the sea."
—Exod. xv. 21.

WHEN God's cloud brings any of his children into a position of
unparalleled difficulty, they may always count upon Him to deliver
them. Our Almighty Parent, like the eagle of which Moses sang
afterwards, delights to conduct the tender nestlings of his care to the
very edge of the precipice, and even to thrust them off into the steeps
of air, that they may learn their possession of unrealized powers of
flight, to be for ever after a luxury; and if, in the attempt, they be
exposed to unwonted peril, He is prepared to swoop beneath them,
and to bear them upward on his mighty pinions.

A conspicuous example of this is given here. From his chariot-
cloud their Almighty Friend looked down upon the cowering crowd
of fugitives in their sore fear as they cried to Him. "In all their
affliction He was afflicted, and the angel of his presence saved them;
in his love and in his pity He redeemed them; and He bare them,
and carried them" throughout that memorable night and day. As
Moses foretold, "He fought for them, while they held their peace."

It would almost seem, from an expression in the Psalms, that the
children of Israel yielded to more rebellion at the Red Sea than
appears from the narrative of Moses. We are told distinctly that they
"provoked him at the Sea, even at the Red Sea, because they remembered not the multitude of his mercies;" so that God saved them in
spite of their rebelliousness, for his Name's sake, and "that He might
make his mighty power to be known" (Psa. cvi. 7, 8). And this
suggests the further thought, that our deliverance does not depend
on our deserts, but upon the Divine purpose. And even though it
might be supposed that our behaviour, in seasons of peril, must
alienate from us the Divine helpfulness, yet it shall not be so; but

notwithstanding all, He will work miracles of power for such as have
no claim on Him, save that which his love gives.

The one man who seemed unmoved amid the panic of the people
was their heroic leader, whose faith was the organ of their deliverance. And therefore it is that in all after-allusions to this great event
his hand is always referred to as the instrument through which the
might of Jehovah wrought. "Thou leddest," says the Psalmist, "thy
people like a flock, by the hand of Moses and Aaron" (Psa. lxxvii.
20). "He caused," says Isaiah, "his glorious arm to go at the right
hand of Moses" (Isa. lxiii. 12, R.V.). The people, therefore, had good
reason to remember the ancient days of Moses; for they were made
famous by Moses' mighty faith. By his faith they passed through the
Red Sea as by dry land.

THE ROD.—There is a limit to prayer. While Moses presented an
appearance of unbroken fortitude towards the people, rearing himself among them like a rock, before God he bent like a broken reed,
crying to Him. That, however, was not the time for heart-rending
supplication, but for action: he must give to the people the word of
advance. Over the sea, on which the shadows of night were falling
rapidly he must stretch out his rod; and by his faith he must afford
the power of God a channel through which it should pass to the
cleavage of the mighty waters.

That rod had already played many parts; it grew first in some
watered glade of the Sinaitic peninsula, little witting of its destiny,
till cut down by the shepherd for the purpose of guiding his flock,
or clubbing some beast of prey; it was in his hand when God first
met with him, and cast upon the ground it became a serpent, emblem
of Egyptian pride. Already it had figured in many of the Egyptian
plagues; stretched over the waters of the river to turn them to blood;
lifted towards heaven to summon the storm; extended over the land
to turn the very dust to lice; hereafter it was to win victory over
Amalek, and to open streams from the heart of the rock; everywhere
emphatically as "the rod of God." But never in all its history had it
done, nor would it do, such marvels as awaited it that night, when at
the bidding of God it was stretched over the waters of the Red Sea.

As the rod was in the hands of Moses, so Moses was in the hand
of God; and so may each of us be, if only we yield ourselves implicitly to Him for service. By nature we may be of the coarsest
texture, not pine, nor oak, nor cedar; by education, we may be
uncultured and unpolished; there may be many notches in us which

mar our symmetry and beauty: but what do these things matter? the one essential is to know that we are being wielded and used by the hands that shaped the worlds, and built the arch of heaven. The glass-blower has beside him on the bench the rudest iron tools to aid him in the execution of the most exquisite designs; but the dexterity of his touch more than compensates for their apparent inaptitude. Be a piece of iron if you will, or a rod cut from the forest tree; but be sure that you are in the right hand of the Master Workman.

THE CLOUD.—Up till now the pillar of cloud had swept in majestic glory through the heavens; but at this juncture it settled down upon the ground like a great wall of billowy vapour, standing for a fence between the camp of Egypt and the camp of Israel. To the former it was dark and menacing, forbidding progress, and enshrouding the movements of the fugitives; to the latter it gave light, casting a sheen upon the sand and sea, and indicating, with unerring accuracy, the path that soon appeared. All night through, those heaven-lit beacon fires shone out; and in after-days the memory of the effect produced by the mingling of their light with the walls of glassy water, supplied the inspired seer with the imagery with which to depict the triumph of the redeemed, who stand on the shores of the "glassy sea mingled with fire, having the harps of God." It seemed as if inspiration itself could find no worthier emblem for that supreme event than the rapture and triumph of the host of Israel on the night, when the glory of the Shechinah flashed back from the crested billows, marshalled on either hand, as the pillared entrance to a mighty temple.

THE PASSAGE.—At this point, following the lead of the Psalmist-historian, it is clear that a terrific storm broke upon the scene. The earth shook and trembled; the massy foundations of the mountains rocked; from out the darkness brooding overhead, the curtains of God's pavilion, came the repeated flash of the lightning, followed by the long reverberation of the thunder. The Most High uttered his voice, which was followed by the pelt of the hailstones and the fall of fireballs. The east wind rose in fury, driving before it the retreating waters, which fled at the blast of the breath of his nostrils; then catching them up in its hands it piled them, wave on wave, until they stood up a wall of foam and tumult, from base to top, fretting, seething, fuming, chafing at the unexpected restraint, and wondering at the unwonted posture, but held steadily and always by the pressure of that mighty blast, that gave them no respite, but held them as in a vice; and all the water behind, backed up, leant upon that rampart, so strangely built, so marvellously maintained.

And on the other side the tide withdrew back and back towards the fountains of the great deep behind. It was as if every wavelet felt the pull, the suction of an abyss opening somewhere far down in the sea, and hastened to fill it, leaving the foundations of the deep naked in the headlong rush. Then the channels of water appeared, the foundations of the world were laid bare, so that rocks and stones deposited in primeval times, and closely veiled from all prying gaze, awoke to find themselves discovered.

Presently it seemed as if there was a pause in the speed of the retreating waters, and they began slowly to return; but as they did so they met with the restraint of the hand of God, which, leaving a pathway of sufficient breadth from the wall already formed, commenced to constitute a second, and "so the flood stood upright as an heap, and the deeps were congealed in the heart of the sea."

Shelving down from the shore between these two walls of water, a broad thoroughfare lay outspread, which the prophet compares to those mountain paths by which cattle descend from the heights on which they graze to the valleys where they rest (Isa. lxiii. 14). Was there ever such a strange comparison? And yet for the moment it seemed almost as natural; and at that moment the word which had sprung from the lips of the leader, and had been caught by those who stood closest around him, passed like prairie fire, though in a whisper, from lip to lip. "Speak unto the children of Israel that they go forward"; and immediately, without precipitate haste, but with glad obedience, the ransomed host stepped down, rank after rank, and passed between the walls of glass and fire amid the rattle of the storm, which made the withdrawal of their hosts inaudible to their foes.

Imagine, O child of God, if you can, that triumphal march: the excited children restrained from ejaculations of wonder by the perpetual hush of their parents; the almost uncontrollable excitement of the women as they found themselves suddenly saved from a fate worse than death; while the men followed or accompanied them, ashamed or confounded that they had ever mistrusted God or murmured against Moses: and as you see those mighty walls of water piled by the outstretched hand of the Eternal in response to the faith of a single man, learn what God will do for his own. Dread not any result of implicit obedience to his command; fear not the angry waters which, in their proud insolence, forbid your progress; fear not the turbulent crowds of men who are perpetually compared to waters lifting up their voice and roaring with their waves. Fear none of these things. Above the voices of many waters, the mighty breakers of the sea, the Lord sits as king upon the flood; yea, the Lord sitteth as king for ever. A storm is only as the outskirts of his robe, the symptom of his advent, the environment of his presence. His way lies through, as well as *in* the sea, his path amid mighty waters, and his footsteps are veiled from human reason. Dare to trust Him; dare to follow Him! Step right down into the ooze of the sea, to find it rock; go down into the mighty depths, to discover that the very forces which barred your progress and threatened your life, at his bidding become the materials of which an avenue is made to liberty.

THE PURSUIT.—As soon as the Egyptians became aware that Israel was escaping, they followed them, and went on after them into the midst of the sea. There was a good deal of pride and obstinacy in this act, which tempted God and presumptuously dared him to do his worst; and, forthwith, when the host was between the walls of water, the whole force of the storm seemed to spend itself on them. The Lord looked upon them through the pillar of fire and of cloud, and troubled them; a sudden panic seized them; their heavy chariots could make but ill progress amid the ooze of the sea bottom, and the wheels themselves became clogged and bound so that they could not move; and they turned to flee, conscious that a greater than Israel was engaged against them.

At this juncture the morning light began to break; and, at the bidding of God, Moses stretched out his hand over the sea from that further shore which he and Israel had by this time gained, and the sea returned to its strength. The Egyptians fled against it in vain; they were overwhelmed in the sudden rush of water toppling down on them from either side. They sank as lead in the mighty waters; they went down like a stone into its depths; and in less time than it takes to tell the story, not a trace of their proud array remained.

THE SONG OF MOSES.—"Then sang Moses." The morning dawn revealed one of the most memorable spectacles of history. A nation of slaves, fleeing from their masters, had suddenly become a nation of freemen, and stood emancipated upon the shores of a new continent. The proud people, which for generations had inflicted such untold griefs upon them, had suffered a humiliation from which it would take them generations to recover. The chivalry of Egypt was overwhelmed in the midst of the sea, there remained not so much as one of them left; and all along the shore lay the bodies of the dead, cast up from the depths of the tide. At this day a significant blank in the hieroglyphed memorials of Egypt tells the story of that overwhelming disaster. And there was given to Israel for all subsequent time an evidence of the trustworthiness of God, which compelled belief, not only in their great Deliverer, but in his servant Moses. It is thus, if only we are still, and commit to Him our cause, that He will vindicate us from the aspersions of our detractors, and bring out our judgment to the light. And we shall look back on the forms which once filled us with dread, dead upon the seashore; unable to pursue or hurt us more.

And from that ransomed host, congregated there in one vast throng, broke forth an anthem, whose sublime conceptions of language rendered it worthy of the occasion, as it had been the model for triumphal songs in all subsequent times.

There is no thought of any but the Lord throughout the entire piece. The song was sung to Him and of Him. It was *He* that had triumphed gloriously, and cast horse and rider into the sea. It was *his* right hand that had dashed in pieces the enemy. It was because *He* blew with *his* wind, that they sank as lead in the mighty waters. It was through the greatness of *his* excellency that they were overthrown who had risen against Him. All the honours of the victory were reverently laid at his feet. Moses is not once referred to.

And the ease of his victory was clearly accentuated. The waters were piled as walls by his breath. He blew with his wind, and a whole army sank as a stone into the depths. He had but to stretch out his right hand, and the sea swallowed the flower of the greatest army of the time.

Note the epithets heaped on God: "My strength and song and salvation;" "glorious in holiness, fearful in praises, doing wonders;" whilst the men extolled Him as "a man of war," and dwelt on the anguish that must take hold of the inhabitants of Canaan when they heard the story of the overthrow. The women, led by Miriam, replied in a noble refrain, "Sing ye to the Lord, for He hath triumphed gloriously; the horse and his rider hath He thrown into the sea."

Whether or not this ode were composed beforehand in anticipation of this moment we cannot tell. It may have been; else how could it have been sung by those assembled thousands? But this in itself would be a striking token of the faith which dwelt so vigorously in the heart of Moses. It was *his* song pre-eminently; and in its closing notes we catch a glimpse of his forecast of the future, and the certainty of his convictions: "Thou shalt bring them in and plant them in the mountain of thine inheritance."

So does God turn our anxieties into occasions of singing— weeping endures for a night, but joy comes in the morning. The redeemed obtain gladness and joy; God puts gladness into their hearts, and new songs into their mouths. Long years of waiting and preparation and obedience shall be rewarded at last, as certainly as God is God. If not before, yet surely when the eternal morning is breaking on the shores of time, we shall join in shouts of victory; which shall awaken eternal echoes, as with myriads beside we sing the song of Moses, the servant of God, and the song of the Lamb.

XIII

Marah and Elim

"All these things happened unto them by way of figure."
—I Cor. x. 11 (r.v., *marg.*)

THE PENINSULA of Sinai, on the shores of which the ransomed people stood, and which for forty years was to be their school-house, is one of the wildest, grandest, barest countries in the world. It has been described as a tangled maze of mountains, piled in inextricable confusion, and gradually rising in height towards the lofty summit of Um-Shomer, to the south of Sinai. Between the Red Sea and the lowest outworks of these mighty citadels of rock there is a plain of gravel; and thence the way climbs slowly upward through long avenues and passes composed of purple granite or brilliant sandstone, which give a richness to the landscape unknown to our bleaker and greyer hills.

We have not now to do with those majestic approaches to the inner sanctuary; but with the sandy plain over which, during the first weeks of wandering, the host was led, skirting the shores of the Red Sea, along which they probably beheld the dead bodies of their foes—a ghastly spectacle !

Though not expressly stated, there must have been a division of the Israelite host, from the point where their first encampments were pitched in the strange new land of freedom. The flocks and herds, as is the custom with modern Arabs, were dispersed far and wide over the country, to crop the scanty "pastures of the wilderness," of which the Psalmist speaks. "Nearly everywhere," Dean Stanley tells us, "there is a thin, it might almost be said a transparent, coating of vegetation. And in some few places there are more marked spots of verdure, the accomplishments, not of the empty beds of winter torrents, but of the few living, perhaps perennial springs; which by the mere fact of their rarity assume an importance difficult to be understood, in the moist scenery of these northern lands." It was there that their flocks and herds were preserved, whilst the main body of the people marched with Moses.

How marvellous the change ! No longer the ceaseless pulse of movement of Egypt, with festival and pageant, song and feast, the court and the army; no longer the green valley of the beneficent Nile, where water never failed, and luscious vegetables, melons, leeks, and garlic, charmed away thirst; no longer the majestic glory of sphinx, and pyramid, and temple: but instead, a silence so intense that the Arabs say they can make their voices heard across the Gulf of Akaba, a waste so waterless, that they might count themselves fortunate if they met a spring in a day's march; whilst they were literally enclosed within a temple, whose walls were stupendous rocks, such as human hands had never piled. But amid all these chequered and strange experiences, the cloud slowly led them forward; and as the successive scenes crowd on our view, we cannot but see in them an allegory or parable of human life, and we acknowledge the truth of the Apostle's statement, "Now these things happened unto them by way of figure" (1 Cor. x. 11, R.V., *marg.*).

I. THE COURAGEOUS FAITH OF MOSES.—He knew that desert well— its wild and desolate character, its dried torrent-beds, its lack of all that would support human life; he knew, too, that if they were to follow the northern route it would not take them very long to reach the land of the Philistines, "which was near," and where they would be easily able to procure all necessary supplies either by force or purchase; but we are told, nevertheless, that he deliberately led them southwards and entered the wilderness. "So Moses brought Israel from the Red Sea, and they went out into the wilderness of Shur." He could not do otherwise, because the cloud went that way; but even with that indication of God's will before his eyes, it must have required an heroic faith to lead two millions of people direct into the wilderness (Exod. xiii. 17; xv. 22).

We all of us need the leading about by the way of the wilderness. In its majestic scenery, our minds, dwarfed and stunted by too great familiarity with the works of men, are turned to a higher keynote, and learn to wonder at the littleness of the vanities which engross so many. There we learn to deal with God not at second-hand, as is too frequent in human civilization; but directly, as scattering with his own hand the manna for our food, and deriving from "the flinty rock" the living streams to quench our thirst. We lose the luxuries which were sapping and enervating our moral nature, to find ourselves becoming braced and strengthened in every sinew by privation and hardship. Patience, freedom, faith, the pilgrim-spirit—all these are children of the wilderness wanderings, that thrive in its rare and peculiar air.

There was good reason, then, why the great leader should follow the lead of the cloud; but it was not the less a sublime evidence of a faith that could trust God to the uttermost, as he turned his back on Philistia, and steadfastly took his course towards the heart of the desert, veiled as yet in those mighty ramparts and walls of rock.

II. The Testing of His Faith.—"They went three days in the wilderness, and found no water" (Exod. xv. 22). The first day's journey was, doubtless, very distressing—the blinding sand-storms; the glare of the sun reflected from the white limestone plains; the absence of shade, of tree, of water. And the water which they carried in their water-skins must have become hot and unrefreshing.

The second day was not less trying. The sea was now far in their rear, and there was nothing to break the monotony of the treeless, lifeless, waterless horizon. And surely as they pitched their black tents for the night, it was difficult to repress some discontent, or at least anxiety, as to what the morrow might bring to their blistered feet and fevered lips. Their supplies of water were also getting low, if they were not quite exhausted.

The third day broke. Perhaps Moses, knowing that pools of water were not far away, encouraged them to persevere; and every eye was eagerly strained to catch the first sight of palm trees and living verdure. Not more eagerly does the mother look for the symptoms of returning life on the cheek of her child, or the beleaguered garrison scan the horizon for the first signal of the relieving squadron, than did those wistful eyes seek for the promised signs.

And when at last, towards the close of the day, they descried them in the far distance, how glad their shouts, how buoyant their hearts, how ready their expressions of confidence in Moses! Their fatigues and complaints and privations were all forgotten, as with quickened pace they made for the margin of the wells. But ah, how great was their disappointment and chagrin when the first long draught filled their mouths with bitterness, and they discovered that the water was too nauseous to drink!

So long as there was none to be got, they had managed to endure; but this sorrow was harder than they could bear, and they turned on Moses and murmured, "What shall we drink?" "They soon forgot His works." From minstrels they became mutineers.

Do we not all know something of the wilderness march? It may follow on some great deliverance. But how great a contrast there is between the rapturous hallelujahs of the one, and the wearying commonplace of the other! The start is both interesting and delightful; but it is so hard to plod on day after day, amid the dust of the shop, the glare of temptation, the pressure of grinding poverty, the routine of irksome toil. The wilderness is no child's play; it is meant to be our school, our training-ground, our arena, where we are being sternly and carefully educated for our great future. And then Marahs will come—bitter disappointments, heart-rending sorrow, as our ideals are shattered and our cherished plans torn to shreds. Ah me! it were better to plod on day by day without the vision of coming bliss, than to awake to discover that it has been an unsubstantial mirage. The Marahs are permitted to prove us, or, in other words, to show what is in us. What pilgrim to the New Jerusalem is there that has not visited those springs, and mingled bitter tears with the bitter waters?

III. MOSES' RESOURCE.—"He cried unto the Lord." How much better this than to rebuke the people, or to threaten to throw up his appointment, or to sit down in despondency as utterly out of heart! The disciples of John, when they had buried their beloved leader, went and told Jesus. And in all ages the servants of God have been glad to turn from their discouragements and the ingratitude of those for whom they would have gladly laid down their lives, to Him whose heart is open to every moan, and whose love is over all and through all, and in all.

Beside each bitter Marah pool there grows a tree, which, when cast into the waters, makes them palatable and sweet. It is so ever. Poison and antidote, infection and cure, pain and medicine, are always close together. The word which saves is nigh even in the mouth and in the heart. We do not always see the "sufficient grace"; but it is there. Too occupied with our disappointment, we have no heart to seek for it; but when we cry, it is shown to our weary longing eyes.

And of what is that tree the type, if not of the cross of Jesus—

which is the symbol, not only of our redemption, but of a yielded will ? It was there that his obedience to the will of his Father reached its supreme manifestation. He became obedient to death, even the death of the cross. Nor is there anything that will so take the bitterness out of disappointment, and so make it palatable and even life-giving, as to look up from it to the cross, and to say, "Not my will, but Thine be done. Thy will is my weal. In Thy will is my bliss."

What a constant lesson Moses was learning from day to day ! God must indeed have become a living reality to him. He learnt God's ways; we are expressly told "that they were made known to him." And gradually he must have come to feel that the whole responsibility of the pilgrimage was on the great, broad shoulders of his Almighty Friend. Ah, fellow-workers, let us not carry the burdens of his responsibilities arising out of his work ! Our one thought should be to be on his track, and to be in living union with Himself. We may leave all the rest with Him.

IV. ELIM.—There are more Elims in life than Marahs; and we *encamp* by them. We are not bidden to tarry at the one, but we may spend long blessed days at the other. How refreshing the shadow of those seventy palm-trees ! How sweet the water of those twelve wells ! How delightful those long restful days ! You say that they will never come to you ? Yes, but they will ! They come to all tired souls. There is no desert-march without an Elim at last. The Lamb cannot fail to lead you by living fountains of water, and to wipe away all tears from your eyes, before you pass the gateway of pearl. A lull comes in the storm; an arbour on the Hill Difficulty; a pause in the march. He makes his sheep to lie down in pastures of tender grass, and leads them beside waters of rest. "Oh, magnify the Lord with me, and let us exalt his name together !"

We must tread the desert, or we can never come to Elim. But the desert lends the Elim much of its bliss. The Castle of Doubting makes the vision from the Delectable Mountains so entrancing. The long illness makes the air so exquisite in the first-permitted walk or drive. The long winter snows paint the fairest colours on the spring flowers. Do not stay murmuring at Marah; press on ! our Elim is within sight. Hope thou in God, for thou shalt yet praise Him.

At Marah Moses received from God a glad, fresh revelation, that God would be the healer of his people in their wilderness march, securing them from the diseases of Egypt. Marvellous that such a message should be sent at such a time ! But the grace of God is not restrained by human sin from making its glad surprises. And Elim was the vindication of the promise. What a God is ours ! He overthrows our foes in the sea, and disciplines his people in the desert. He leads us over the burning sand, and rests us in luxuriant glades. He permits disappointment at Marah, and surprises us at Elim. He leads us by a cloud ; but He speaks to us by a human voice. He counts the number of the stars ; but He feeds his flock like a shepherd, and gently leads those that give suck. He chooses a thundercloud as the canvas on which He paints his promise in rainbow hues. He proves by Marah, and at Elim recruits us.

XIV

The Gift of Manna

"When the dew that lay was gone up, behold, upon the face of the wilderness a small round thing, small as the hoar frost on the ground. And when the children of Israel saw it, they said one to another, What is it? for they wist not what it was. And Moses said unto them, It is the bread which the Lord hath given you to eat."

—Exod. xvi. 14–16 (R.V.).

WE MAY encamp at Elim, and stay for long happy days in its green bowers, but we may not live there; at least the majority may not. It is so much harder, and needs so much more grace, to remain devoted and earnest, to retain the girt loin and the soldier-like bearing, in its soft, enervating climate, than on the bare and sterile sand of the desert, with its rare and stimulating air. Few characters are able to reach their highest and noblest excellence amid the genial conditions through which at times each life is permitted to pass. Therefore it is that, though the cloud of the Divine guidance broods at Elim long enough to recruit us, it soon gathers up its folds, and commences its majestic progress over the desert expanse, leaving us no alternative but to strike our tents and follow. So it is said that "they took their journey from Elim; and all the congregation of the children of Israel came unto the wilderness of Sin, which is between Elim and Sinai" (ver. 1).

Farewell to the seventy palm-trees and the twelve water-springs! Farewell to the brief, bright hours of respite from the blinding glare of the desert! But He whose nature was mirrored in that exquisite beauty, who was able to reproduce any number of Elims if He chose—*He* could never be left behind, but always must accompany his people.

It is immaterial whether He locates us amid verdure or desert. He is responsible to make up from his own resources for that which is lacking in outward circumstance. What if there are no palm-trees?

The shadow of the Almighty must be our shelter from the sultry heat.

There are things about God, and his ability to supply all needs of the soul of man, which could not be learnt in any Elim, with all its beauty; and can only be acquired where its bowers are exchanged for those long corridors of rock which lead to the foot of Sinai, as the ancient approaches of obelisks conducted to the pillared halls of Karnak. The eagle-wings on which God bears his people are only spread beneath them when the nest is broken up and left. The supremacy of God over all natural laws is only learnt when they are seen to stand before Him as the angels who do his bidding, hearkening unto the voice of his word. The patient tenderness of God, the motherside of his nature, is only apparent where a whole host breaks out into the sobbings of a querulous child. The punctuality of God is more easily discerned in the spread breakfast-table of the wilderness than in the procession of the seasons or the march of worlds. It is well, then, to leave Elim; beyond it lie Sinai, Pisgah, and Canaan.

I. THE DESERT MURMURINGS.—It was a great aggravation of the responsibilities which already lay heavily on the heart of Moses, to have to encounter the perpetual murmurings of the people whom he loved so well. It only drove him continually back on his Almighty Friend and Helper, to pour into his most tender and sympathizing ear the entire tale of sorrow. But the repeated outbreak of these murmurings all along the wilderness route only sets in more conspicuous prominence the beauty of his gentle meekness, and the glory of his faith, which probably was the one channel through which the power of God wrought for the salvation and blessing of his people.

The race of murmurers is, alas! not extinct. Lips which have joined in singing consecration hymns, sometimes give passage to complaints. And we are none of us so careful as we ought to be to restrain the expression of discontent. How often are murmurings mingled with the food we eat, because we are not exactly pleased with its quality or preparation; with the weather, because it does not quite fit in with our plans; with our daily calling, because it is irksome and distasteful; and with the presence or absence of certain persons in our lives!

Murmurers are short of Memory. It was only one short month

since the people had come forth out of Egypt—a month crowded
with the wonders which the right hand of the Lord had wrought.
The chronicler specially notes that it was the fifteenth day of the
second month, and adds, "The whole congregation of the children
of Israel murmured against Moses and Aaron in the wilderness; and
the children of Israel said unto them, Would to God we had died
by the hand of the Lord in the land of Egypt, when we sat by the
flesh-pots, and when we did eat bread to the full; for ye have brought
us forth into this wilderness to kill this whole assembly with hunger"
(verses 2 and 3).

They could remember very well the sensual delights of Egypt; but
they forgot the lash of the taskmaster, and the anguish of heart with
which they wrought at the kneading of the clay. They forgot how
graciously God had provided for their needs ever since they had
stood around their tables to eat the flesh of the paschal lamb. They
forgot the triumph-song, which recorded their undoubting faith that
God would bring them in and plant them in the land of their inheritance. None of these things availed to stay the torrent of their murmuring complaint.

Whenever a murmuring fit threatens, let us review the past, and
recount the Lord's dealings with us in bygone years. Did He deliver
in six troubles, and is He likely to forsake us in the seventh? Has He
ransomed our souls from the power of the grave, and will He not
regard the body, which is included in the purchase-money? When the
Psalmist complained, and his spirit was overwhelmed, he tells us that
he considered the days of old, the years of ancient times; he called to
remembrance his song in the night; he remembered the years of the
right hand of the Most High. "I will remember the works of the
Lord; surely I will remember thy wonders of old." And as at the
summons of memory, the sea of the past gives up its dead, each risen
record of God's goodness will condemn the murmur, and rally the
wavering faith.

Murmurers are short of Sight. They fail to see that behind all the
appearances of things there lie hid the Presence and Providence of
God. Moses called the attention of the people to this fact, which
enhanced so gravely the magnitude of their offence. They thought
that they were only venting their spleen on a man like themselves.
Annoyed and apprehensive, it was some relief to expend their spleen
on the one man to whom they owed everything. Ah! how vain it is
to trust the populace, which to-day cries Hosanna; to-morrow,

Crucify! But their faithful leader showed them that their insults were directed not against himself, but against Him whose servant he was, and at whose bidding everything was being wrought. "The Lord heareth your murmurings which ye murmur against HIM; and what are we? Your murmurings are not against us, but against the Lord" (ver. 8).

It becomes us to ponder well those words. Some of God's children are more willing to admit a general providence than a special particular one. But the former involves the latter. The whole teaching of Jesus compels us to believe in a care which counts the hairs of our heads. The very necessities of our education demand a Divine superintendence of the insignificances and commonplaces of life. God must be in all things, ordaining and permitting them. It is impossible, therefore, to grumble, without the sword of our words cutting through the gauze-like drapery of what we see, and wounding Him whom circumstances scarcely avail to hide. Grumblings, murmurings, complaints, these are directed against the will and arrangement and plan of God. And their cure is to accept all things from his hand, to acquiesce in his wise appointments, and to believe that He is securing the very best results.

Murmurers are Short of Faith. The pressure of want had begun to make itself felt but very slightly, if at all, on the host. It was not so much the hardship that they were at that moment experiencing, but that which they thought to be imminent. Provisions were running short; supplies were becoming exhausted; the slender store refused to be eked out beyond a comparatively short period. It was thus that they came to Moses and murmured.

God often delays his help. He tarries ere He comes, long enough to bring us to the end of ourselves, and to show the futility of looking for creature aid. At such times we too often evade the lesson which He would teach, and bemoan our hard lot, though it is only a suggestion of our fearful hearts. From the marshy swamps of our inner life arises the miasma of unbelief, in the folds of which our imagination affects to descry gaunt and fearful objects; and immediately we think that they have, or will have, a real existence, we fall straightway all along on the earth, and are sore afraid, as Saul before the ghost of Samuel.

Too many of God's children despond because of what they dread, and break out into murmurings that they are going to be killed; when if they were to stop to think for a single moment, they would see that God is pledged by the most solemn obligations to provide for them. Why do you murmur ? It is because you doubt. Why do you doubt ? It is because you will look out on the future, or consider your circumstances, apart from God. But when the eye is single in its steadfast gaze towards Him—his love, his wisdom, his resources—faith grows strong, reads his love in his eyes, reckons on his faithfulness, and realizes that He who spared not his own Son, but delivered Him up for us all, will with Him also freely give us all things.

How different to this murmuring life was that of our blessed Lord, who also was led into the wilderness, and was without food for forty days ! But He did not complain ; no word of murmuring passed his lips, although He might have remonstrated with the Father for dealing thus with one who had always yielded Him a prompt and glad obedience. And even when He hungered, and the devil suggested that hunger was not becoming to the newly-designated Son of God, He meekly said that it was enough for Him to have his Father's will. He was prepared for all that it might involve. He insisted that if God withheld bread, He would sustain the body He had made in some other way. The Son never for a moment questioned his Father's right to follow any line of procedure He chose, and was apparently perfectly satisfied. He had learnt the secret of how to be full and to be hungry, how to abound and to suffer need. He did not live by bread alone ; but by every word that proceeded out of the mouth of God. And in this Divine patience He has shown how murmuring may find no foothold, and how the soul may be braced to endure hardship.

II. THE WILDERNESS FOOD.—It is not for us to tell here the whole story of the manna, with its wealth of spiritual reference to the true Bread, which is Christ. It is enough to remember :

To look up for our supplies. "He gave them bread from heaven to eat." For the believer there are five sources from which help may come ; for in addition to the four quarters of the winds he looks up to the heavens. There came *from heaven* the sound of the rushing of a mighty wind. Look higher, child of God, to the heart and hand of the Father !

To feed on the heavenly bread daily and early. "They gathered it every morning, and when the sun waxed hot it melted." There is no time like the early morning hour for feeding on the flesh of Christ by communion with Him, and pondering his words. Once lose tha t, and the charm is broken by the intrusion of many things, though it may be they are all useful and necessary. You cannot re-make the broken reflections of a lake swept by wind. How different is that day from all others, the early prime of which is surrendered to fellowship with Christ! Nor is it possible to live to-day on the gathered spoils of yesterday. Each man needs all that a new day can yield him of God's grace and comfort. It must be daily bread.

To feed on Christ is the only secret of strength and blessedness. If only believers in Christ would realize and appropriate the lesson so clearly taught in this narrative, as well as in the wonderful discourse which our Lord founded upon it (John vi. 22–58), they would find themselves the subjects of a marvellous change. It is almost incredible how great a difference is wrought by the prolonged and loving study of what the Scriptures say concerning Him. To sit down to enjoy them; to read two or three chapters, an epistle, or a book, at a sitting; to let the heart and mind steep in it; to do this before other intruders have noisily entered the heart and distracted its attention—ah, how this transforms us!

We close this chapter, however, by calling attention to the remarkable expression used by our Lord, when He said, "Moses gave you not that bread from heaven" (John vi. 32); intimating that though Moses did not give that eternal Bread of which He was speaking, yet he did give some sort of bread, *i.e.*, the manna: so that there was a sense in which the faithful servant procured and gave daily the provision on which his people fed.

We are not unfamiliar, in these days, with instances in which the faith of one man avails to procure the daily food of hundreds of orphans and of others. God gives to them that they may give to those with whom they are charged. But all these are dwarfed before the stupendous miracle of a faith that was capable of covering the desert place with food for forty years!

No one who reads these words need ever hesitate to enter into partnership with God for any enterprise to which the Almighty may summon him. The only thing that is at all necessary is to be quick to catch the faintest expression of his will, prompt to obey, and strong to persevere. When these conditions are fulfilled, the soul walks with God in blessed companionship; taking pleasure in difficulty, straitness, famine, and peril, because each of these becomes a foil for the display of the Divine resources, who makes even mountains a way. Such an one is perfectly indifferent to murmuring or applause, to censure or praise; since the soul is engrossed with a companionship which is perfect bliss, because perfect satisfaction.

Let us, then, unceasingly make our boast in the Lord, as we step out on to the unknown and untried. And who shall lament the beauty of Elim, or the fleshpots of Egypt, or the frugal meals of Jethro's tent, when such lessons are to be learnt in the society of our eternal Friend, who can never fail those who dare to trust Him; and who gives to the uttermost capacity of our faith, that we may in turn give as much as they need to those poor friends of ours, who knock us up with entreaties for help and bread (Luke xi. 5–9).

XV

REPHIDIM

"And there was no water for the people to drink. And the Lord said, Thou shalt smite the rock, and there shall come water out of it. And Moses did so.

"Then came Amalek and fought with Israel in Rephidim. . . . And Moses' hands were steady until the going down of the sun. . . . And Moses built an altar and called the name of it JEHOVAH-NISSI—The Lord my banner."

—EXOD. xvii. 1–15.

IF YOU essay to lead men, you will sooner or later come to a Rephi dim. We are distinctly told that it was according to the command-ment of the Lord that the children of Israel journeyed "by stages" (ver. 1, R.V., *marg.*) from the wilderness of Sin, and pitched in Rephidim. The character of the worker is as dear to God as the work he is doing; and no pains must be spared by the Divine Artificer to complete the design to which He has set his hand. Do not be surprised then, Christian worker, if you find yourself landed in Rephidim. There are lessons to be learnt there of incalculable worth.

Geographers and historians have found it difficult to fix on its precise locality; but the site is immaterial. It lay, no doubt, some-where along that coast in one of the wadys that lead up into the heart of the mountains of the central table-land. But the experiences of which that place was the scene are common to all lives, ages, and lands.

I. THERE WE LEARN THE LIMIT OF OUR ABILITY.—Few of us can stand great or long-continued success. It is comparatively easy to walk in the Valley of Humiliation, when our path is hidden and the faces of men are averted; but to stand on the height, with none to rival, with nothing left to scale, the wonder and the envy of a host—ah! this is a task in which the brain reels, the step falters, and the heart gets proud. It is easier to know how to be abased than how to

abound, how to be empty than how to be full. We are so apt to
repeat the folly of Hezekiah in showing his treasures to the ambassa-
dors of Babylon; and to utter the mad vaunt of Nebuchadnezzar,
"Is not this great Babylon which *I* have built, by the might of my
power, and for the glory of my majesty!"

But whenever this happens, directly the heart of man is inflated
with pride, and lifts itself up in self-confidence, there is an end to its
usefulness. God will not give his glory to another. He will not
permit his power to be employed for the inflation of human pride, or
to minister to the exaltation of the flesh. It is his solemn decree that
no flesh shall glory in his presence. "Shall the axe boast itself against
him that heweth therewith? shall the saw magnify itself against him
that shaketh it? as if the rod should shake itself against them that
lift it up" (Isa. x. 15).

This is why so many of God's servants, who once did yeoman
service, are laid aside. They were marvellously helped till they were
strong; but when they were strong, their hearts were lifted up to their
destruction. They still preach the old sermons that once pealed like
the archangel's trumpet, or thrilled with the wail of Calvary's broken
heart; but there is no stir or shaking among the dry bones that strew
the valley of vision. They utter the old exorcisms; but the demons
laugh at them from behind their ramparts, and refuse to go forth.
They know that the Lord has departed from them, and that it is not
with them as in the days that are past. If such would only consider
and search their hearts, they would find that they had commenced
to trust in the momentum of past success; and to think that somehow
the draught of fishes was due to their own fisher-experience, instead
of being the direct gift of One who often traverses all the rules of
art by a Divine knowledge and power.

We can easily suppose that Moses was in danger of a similar fall.
For the last few months his career had been an uninterrupted line of
success. He had brought the proudest monarch of his time to his
knees with the cry of a suppliant. He had become very great in the
eyes of priesthood and court. He had led the greatest Exodus the
world had seen or would see. The parted ocean, the submerged host,
the song of victory, the fall of the manna, the evidence of his states-
manship and sagacity as a born leader of men—all combined to place
him in an unparalleled position of authority and glory. As the
triumphal ode puts it, "He was king in Jeshurun, when the heads
of the people were gathered" (Deut. xxxiii. 5).

Was there no temptation in all this? Men warn others against temptations on which they have been at the point of sliding to their fall; and may it not have been from his own experience that Moses derived the caution given to the people, "Beware that thou forget not the Lord thy God ... lest when all that thou hast is multiplied, thine heart be lifted up, and thou forget the Lord thy God ... and thou say in thine heart, My power and the might of mine hand hath gotten me this wealth" (Deut. viii. 11–17).

Great and good men are not proof against these attacks of pride and vainglory. We are none of us free from the tendency to sacrifice to our net, and burn incense to our drag, because by them our portion is fat, and our meat plenteous. It was for this reason that Paul gloried in his infirmities; finding in them perpetual reminders of his weakness, which kept him low enough for God to choose him as the platform for the putting forth of his might.

It was probably, therefore, that God brought Moses to Rephidim to counteract and check all uprisings of self-sufficiency; to bring him down to the dust of abject helplessness; to teach him the narrow limits of his resources and ability. Lo, all these things doth God work, "That He may withdraw man from his purpose, and hide pride from man" (Job xxxiii. 17).

Whatever Moses may have begun to think, all self-confidence must have vanished like a wreath of mist among the hills when he found himself face to face with that infuriated mob; who broke through every barrier erected by gratitude, or patriotism, or self-respect, or memory of past deliverances, and with violence demanded water. "The people did chide with Moses, and said, Give us water that we may drink ... And the people murmured against Moses, and said, Wherefore hast thou brought us up out of Egypt, to kill us and our children and our cattle with thirst?" (Exod. xvii. 2, 3). And such was their irritation that they seemed ready to stone him.

Was this the way that they repaid his unstinted service for them? Did they not care for him more than this? Ah, he was not king of their hearts, as he had thought and hoped! And as for water, whence could he procure it? No wisdom or power of his could help in such a strait. Nothing that he could suggest would meet the case. He was absolutely at the end of himself; and "he cried unto the Lord, saying, What shall I do?"

It is a blessed position to which the providence of God reduces us when we find ourselves face to face with an overmastering

necessity. Were it a brook, we might ford it; but here is a river !
Were it the thirst of a little child, we might quench it; but here are
two millions of thirsty souls ! Were it for the water of earth's wells,
we might begin to build aqueducts from the lakes that lie in the
bosom of the hills; but here is thirst for the living water, which
issues from the throne of God and the Lamb ! Then we learn the
limit of our sufficiency. We cry, Who is sufficient for these things ?
And we confess that we are not sufficient of ourselves, to account
anything as from ourselves; but our sufficiency is from God. We
cannot make a revival; or save a soul; or convince a heart of sin, or
break it down in contrition; we cannot comfort, or counsel, or
satisfy the parching thirst. And when we have reached the end of
self, we have got to the beginning of God. It is from the low threshold of the door that the life-giving stream gushes on its heaven-
sent way.

II. THERE WE LEARN MUCH ABOUT GOD.—This always follows
the other lesson. We are brought to know ourselves that we may be
prepared to know God. The Master always says, "Whence are we
to buy bread, that these may eat ? how many loaves have ye ?" not
because He needs the information; but because He desires to bring
his workers face to face with the utter inadequacy of their supply,
and to prepare them better to appreciate the greatness of his power.
But that question, eliciting the fewness of the loaves, is invariably
followed by the demand, "Bring them hither to Me"; and by the
heaps of broken victuals, evidence of the abundance of the supply.
So at Rephidim the need which abases us and drives us to God,
reveals God.

We learn his patience. Not a word of reproach or remonstrance
breaks upon the still desert air. If the people had been exemplary
in their humble trust, they could not have met with more tender
willingness to supply their need. The people, and perhaps Levi
especially, proved Him at Massah, and strove with Him at the waters
of Meribah, asking whether the Lord were among them or not,
though the cloud brooded overhead, and the manna lay each morning around the camp: yet there was no word of rebuke, only directions for the immediate supply of their need. It is only at Rephidim
that we learn his patience towards ourselves and towards others;
because He will ever be mindful of his covenant. "His mercy
endureth for ever."

We learn the reality of his spiritual presence. "I will stand before thee upon the rock in Horeb" (ver. 6). The people had just threatened to stone Moses; but God, in effect, bade him not to fear. It was as if He said, "Fear not, I am with thee; be not dismayed, I am thy God: none shall set on thee to hurt thee, for I am with thee to deliver thee. Pass on before them, thou shalt take no harm; and this shall be a sign that I am actually there upon the rock, it shall gush with watersprings." Never before had God been more real to his servant than he was that day, when He rose up as a rampart to protect him from the infuriated crowd with their threatening stones. It is when men turn against us most, that the Lord stands beside, as He did to Paul, and says, Fear not!

We learn God's secret storehouses. "Thou shalt smite the rock, and there shall come water out of it." This is strange! A rock would seem the last place to choose for the storage of water. But God's cupboards are in very unlikely places. Ravens bring food. The Prime Minister of Egypt gives corn. Cyrus lets go the people of Israel from Babylon. The Jordan heals the leper. Meal makes poisoned pottage wholesome. Wood makes iron swim. A Samaritan binds up the wounds and saves the life of the pillaged traveller. Joseph of Arimathæa buries the sacred body in his own new tomb. It is worth while to go to Rephidim to get an insight into the fertility and inventiveness of God's providence. There can be no lack to them that fear Him, and no fear of lack to those who have become acquainted with his secret storehouses. "Eye hath not seen, nor ear heard . . . the things which God hath prepared for them that love him; but God hath revealed them unto us by his Spirit" (1 Cor. ii. 9, 10).

That smitten rock was a type of Christ. A Rock, indeed!—stable amid upheavel, permanent amid change. A smitten Rock! Reproach broke his heart, and the soldier's spear set abroach the blood and water, which have issued to heal the nations and quench their thirst. "They drank of that spiritual Rock that followed them, and that Rock was Christ." There is no water that will so satisfy thirst as this crystal Rock-water. "Rock of Ages, cleft for me."

III. THERE WE LEARN THE POWER OF PRAYER.—The tribe of Amalek was probably descended from Esau; and, like him, was wild and fierce and warlike. Were they likely tamely to submit to the intrusion of a new people into their pasture-lands and fastnesses, which they had succeeded in holding against Egypt? It was impossible; and so, according to Josephus, this powerful tribe gathered to this spot all the forces of the desert, from Petra to the Mediterranean; and "they smote the hindmost of the Israelites, even all that were feeble among them, when they were faint and weary."

If Egypt represents the power of darkness, Amalek is a type of the flesh; which, though thoroughly defeated and broken, is always apt to crop up in moments of weakness and unwatchfulness. Far down the history of Israel, Haman, the Amalekite, had nearly compassed the annihilation of the whole people. It is in keeping with this typology that Saul was commissioned utterly to destroy the Amalekites; and that Jehovah solemnly pledged Himself to have war with Amalek from generation to generation.

Moses, now eighty-one years old, shrank from the brunt of the battle. He entrusted the troops to Joshua, here first brought into prominence, whilst he climbed the hill, with the sacred rod in his hand. Thence he surveyed the battle, and stretched out his hands in prayer—fought with unseen combatants the livelong day, and won the victory by intercessions, of which those steady arms were the symbol. It is a most beautiful picture. Three old men in prayer. Two staying up the third!

In Rephidim we learn the lesson that prayer will do what else were impossible. In earlier days Moses would never have thought of winning a battle save by fighting. He now learns that he can win it by praying. Probably Paul, too, learnt that lesson in his long and wearisome imprisonments. How they must at first have chafed his eager spirit; accustomed as he was to gird himself, and go whither he would. He may have even been tempted to feel that all his power to affect the destiny of the Church was at an end; when he suddenly discovered a leverage by which he was able to secure greater results than ever; and henceforth each epistle contains a reference to his prayers. Remember his recurring phrase, "I never cease to make mention of you in my prayers."

We cannot compare ourselves with either of these, save as Lilliputians might with a Gulliver; and yet we may, at least, emulate them in their intercessions. According to the prayers of a church are the successes of a church. Are they maintained, the banner floats on to victory: are they languid and depressed, the foe achieves a transient success. Let us, then, learn to pray, filling our Rephidims with strong crying and tears, obtaining by faith for ourselves and others victories which no prowess of our own could win. These shall encourage us like nothing beside, filling our heart with joy, our lips with songs, and our hands with the spoil of the foe. What deliverances might we win for our dear ones, and all others who are strongly molested by the flesh, if only we were more often found on the top of the hill with the uplifted rod of prayer in our steadied hands ! Let then the Christ who is in thee, plead through thee for his Peters, that their faith may not fail; but that they may be saved as birds from the snare of the fowler.

XVI

The God-ward Aspect

"Be thou for the people God-ward, that thou mayest bring the causes
unto God."

—Exod. xviii. 19.

When the Israelite host had left Rephidim, they began to climb up
from the coast of the Red Sea into the heart of the mountain range
of Sinai. Their route has been compared to a stair of rock. Before
them, through the pure air, floated the majestic cloud, leading them
they knew not whither. They only knew that they had no option
but to follow, since their supply of manna and water depended on
absolute obedience to its movement. On either side rose the cliffs of
red sandstone, like the walls of some mighty temple, to the Holy of
Holies of which they were ever approaching. It was apparently on
the route that the incident reported in this chapter took place. For
the words, "at the mount of God," probably refer to the entire
region.

Tidings in the desert fly fast; and the aged priest, in the fastnesses
of Midian, had been kept fully informed of the wonderful series of
events of which his relative had been the centre. When, therefore,
tidings came of the arrival of the vast host in the vicinity of Sinai, he
took Zipporah, Moses' wife, and her two sons, who had been
entrusted to his care, and brought them unto Moses. After the customary profuse Oriental salutations, they spoke long and admiringly
of the way in which the Lord had led his people. And the day closed
with a solemn feast and sacrifice. The morrow seems to have been a
rest day. The cloud did not move forward, but remained stationary;
as if moored by an invisible cable, and spreading itself out as a
refreshing canopy from the burning heat of the sun. And on that
day an incident took place which was destined to have important
issues on the history of the great leader as well as of the people whom
he led. "It came to pass on the morrow that Moses sat to judge the

people; and the people stood by Moses from the morning unto the evening" (ver. 13).

Moses' Habitual Practice.—We get a sudden glimpse here into the kind of life which Moses at this time was leading. When the host encamped, and there was a day at liberty from the weariness of the march, he seems to have sat on a judgment-seat, to which all the people came who had any disputes, or grievances, or matters about which they desired to obtain advice and Divine counsel. Despite all their murmurings they looked upon him as the organ for the voice of God, and sought from his lips an authoritative declaration of the Divine will. To use his own words, when the people had a matter, they came unto him to inquire of God ; and he made them know the statutes of God and his laws.

It was a Divine work, sufficient to engross his noblest powers, and to tax resources which had been stored up within him through long years of waiting ; for what is higher in all this world than to serve as the interpreter of whom Job speaks, "One among a thousand, to show unto man what is right for him ?" (Job xxxiii. 23, R.V.) To hear the difficulties, perplexities, and hard questions of the anxious and troubled ; to inquire for them to God ; to bring their causes to his bar for judgment, and to his mercy-seat for help : to come back to them to teach them, to show them the way in which they should walk, and the work they should do—this is employment which were worthy of the delicacy and strength of an angel's love, and most nearly approaches the ministry of the Redeemer. This blessed work of mediatorship was not borne by Moses as a Priest, for as yet the Priesthood was not constituted ; but as a large-hearted, noble man, who was at leisure from himself, and had the ear of God. He was "for the people to God-ward." And it opens up a very interesting vista of service for us all, especially for those who are intimate with the King, and habituated to the royal Court. Why should we not enter more largely into participation with Moses in this delightful service, which is open to those who are slow of speech equally as to those who are golden-mouthed ; and affords opportunities for the very powers which most shrink from the glare of publicity and the gaze of men?

We can imagine him going to God each day with long lists of questions for one and another of the mighty host. This and the other cause he laid before Him for counsel, quoting names and circumstances, arguments and reasons on either side, and waiting

for the message which he was to carry back. What variety! What
directness! What reality must have pervaded his prayers! How
vividly must he have realized that he was, indeed, in partnership
with the Most High, a fellow-worker and yoke-fellow ; and that
they had a common interest in the people whom they loved! Why
should not we also begin to live such a life? The voice that spake
to him speaks to us, "Be thou for the people to God-ward, that
thou mayest bring the causes unto God" (ver. 19). And the
gates through which he passed and repassed stand open day and
night.

We often wonder at Luther, who spent three hours each day
in prayer and meditation ; at Bishop Andrewes, spending the
greater part of five hours every day in fellowship with God ; at
John Welsh, who thought that day ill spent which did not witness
eight or ten hours of closet communion. It seems to us as if such
prolonged praying must involve an endless monotony of vain
repetitions. We forget that when men are sent to market with a
host of commissions from their neighbours and friends, they must
needs tarry longer than when they go only for themselves. It would
be a very wholesome thing if the causes of others were to detain
us more constantly before the Lord.

This " being for the people to God-ward" became more and more
characteristic of the life of Moses. Whenever the people cried unto
him, he prayed unto the Lord. When the spirit of revolt spread
through the camp, he fell upon his face. When it seemed likely that
the whole nation must perish for their sin, he stood in the breach,
and besought the Lord, and turned away the destruction that hung
over them like a lurid cloud. Twice for forty days their interests
detained him in the holy mount. And in long after years he is
classed with Samuel as one who had stood before God for his
people.

What a striking type is this of our Lord Jesus, though at the best
there is a marvellous gulf between the two. For Moses was faithful
over God's household as a servant ; but Christ as a Son, whose
house are we. All that Moses did He will do, and more. When we
have a matter, let us go to Him. He is for us to God-ward, and will
bring our causes to God. Through Him we may inquire of God ;
and he will make us know (for the responsibility of *making* us know
is on Him, and if one way will not suffice we may trust Him to
adopt another) the statutes of God and his laws ; and will show

us the way in which we should walk, and the work that we must do.

The Tax on Moses' Strength.—Work like this cannot be done without severe expenditure of all that is most vital to man. It drains the sympathies, taxes the brain, wearies the heart charged with the anxieties and sorrows, the burdens and needs of a throng of perplexed and troubled souls. You cannot save others and save yourself as well. Virtue cannot go forth to heal without your becoming conscious of the drain. You can only comfort others when you understand them ; and you cannot understand them till you have given yourself away to them. But the effort to do this costs you all that you are worth to some other soul. And it therefore became apparent to the keen eye of Jethro's loving solicitude that both Moses and the people were being worn away in his attempt to meet all their demands.

In after years Moses himself seems to have broken down under the burden. "And Moses said unto the Lord, Wherefore hast Thou afflicted thy servant? and wherefore have I not found favour in thy sight, that Thou layest the burden of all this people upon me? Have I conceived all this people ? Have I begotten them, that Thou shouldst say unto me, Carry them in thy bosom, as a nursing father beareth the sucking child, unto the land which Thou swarest unto their fathers ?" (Num. xi. 11, 12.) Moses did not feel that strain now when Jethro spoke, for it was as yet fresh on him ; but it was, nevertheless, sapping his strength, and Jethro remarked it.

We do not always see the cost at which we are doing our work. We are sustained by the excitement and interest of it. The stir, the rush, the cry of the combatants, the chances and opportunities of the battle, the alluring form of victory, to be won at the price of just one more effort—all these things conceal from us the expenditure of our reserves, which is patent enough to others. Some men get weary of forbearing ; they cannot live slowly ; they must expend themselves, pouring their lives out as a libation from a bowl. And it is an act of benevolence when some Jethro is prompted to interpose and suggest a mitigation of the fever, a slackening of the eager rush. The Jethros seldom prevail with us. They get scant thanks for their pains. We have to learn by some terrible collapse. But they have, at least, deserved well by us.

From man, breaking down under the weight of human care imposed on his heart by his fellows, let us turn to the true Priest and Brother of Man ; into whose ear is being poured one incessant stream of complaint and sorrow, of care and need, and sin. It is as if all the letters, deposited in all the receiving boxes of England year by year, were directed to one man, who must open and answer them all himself. But even that illustration gives an utterly inadequate idea of all that devolves on our dear Master, Christ, whose heart is the receptacle of all the anguish, sorrow, and soul-travail of mankind.

Moses' patience lasted for a few months only ; but His till the work is done (Deut. i. 31 ; Isa. lxiii. 9 ; Acts xiii. 18, R.V.). He faints not, neither is weary ; because He combines with a woman's sympathy and delicacy of touch and insight, all the patience and strength of the Divine. But do we sufficiently realize the cost at which, through the ages, He is exercising his ministry on our behalf? Think ye not that the festal processions of the glorified often halt upon their way, like that which stayed on the shoulder of Olivet, because the king is in tears! He is "touched with the feeling of our infirmities."

Moses' Assent to Jethro's Proposal.—It cannot be God's will that any of his servants should wear away. He knows our frame too well to overtax its frail machinery. No hard task-master is He, driving his slaves beyond the limit of human endurance. The burden of responsibility which He lays upon their shoulders may be heavy ; but it is not too heavy. The engagements which He assigns for each day may be many ; but not too many for its working hours. The souls committed to their charge may be numbered by thousands ; but they are not more than can be overlooked and shepherded. The bell never summons a servant to a duty concerning which God does not say to him, My grace is sufficient for thee ; as thy day so shall thy strength be.

Sometimes God's workers make the mistake of burdening themselves with work which others could do as well as themselves, and indeed, would be the better for doing. This seems to have been the case with Moses. He appeared to think that he alone could judge, manage, and administer the affairs of Israel. And this monopoly of the administration was working adversely. It was overtaxing himself ; it was wearing out the people; it was delaying the course of justice; and it was allowing a large amount of talent to lie unused. Jethro's advice was therefore most timely, that he should provide out of all the people able men, with the three important qualifications, that they should fear God, love truth, and hate unjust gain. These were to deal with the small matters, whilst the greater ones were still brought to himself.

MOSES has been blamed for doing this. It has been said that if he had trusted God, the power which was now to be divided among many might have been concentrated on himself; so that he might have continued to bear the responsibility and honour of judgment alone. God could have enabled him to do all the work which these others were now to divide with him.

But, surely, even if that had been the case—and we would not for a moment dispute that it could have been so—yet, it would not have been so well as the division of interest and labour which now took place. It was much better to set all these men to work than to do all their work. It evoked talent ; it ennobled them by placing them in positions of responsibility before their fellows; it drove them to personal dealings with God; it inspired them with a fellow-feeling with Moses; it turned critics into sympathizers and companions; it educated them for positions for which they might be required in the emergencies of the future. It is a great matter to be a good workman, one not needing to be ashamed; but it is a greater to be able to call out other workmen, and to set them at work.

This policy was that which the apostles adopted when the business of the Church had so grown upon their hands as to engross too much of their time and energy. They could no longer combine the serving of tables with the ministry of the Word; and as they could not hesitate which side of their double office to abandon, they called in the help of Stephen and his colleagues "to serve tables," whilst they gave themselves to prayer and to the ministry of the Word.

Is there not a thought here for many of the Lord's workers who may read these words ? Are we not dissipating our energies over too wide an area ? Do we not attempt to embrace in our life many things which others could do as well as ourselves ? Ought not those specially, who are gifted with the power of prayer and spiritual insight, to cultivate those special sides of their nature, leaving details of management and direction of finance to others ? We should live on the greatest side of our nature, reserving ourselves for that; not careless of minor details, if there is no one else to manage them; but prepared to hand them over to "able men," even though they may have to learn their duties at a cost, in the beginning, of some mistakes and failures. The mountain brow, with its fellowship, affords a leverage from which we may best move earth. We touch men most when we most touch God. The prophet and priest, the man of God, the teacher, these are among the choicest gifts of God to men. And if you are gifted specially in these directions, cultivate such endowments to the uttermost—they are rare enough—leaving other details to be cared for by others who may be cast in a more practical mould.

XVII

AT THE FOOT OF SINAI

"And Mount Sinai was altogether on a smoke, because the Lord descended
upon it in fire: and the smoke thereof ascended as the smoke of a furnace,
and the whole mount quaked greatly."
—EXOD. xix. 18.

FROM Rephidim the children of Israel marched slowly and laboriously
through the great thoroughfare of the desert now known as the
Wady-es-Sheykh, the longest, widest, and most continuous of those
vast desert valleys. It must have been an astonishing exchange from
the flat alluvial land of Egypt, where the only hills were those raised
by the hands of man. On either side of the pilgrim host lofty and
precipitous mountains reared their inaccessible ramparts of red
sandstone and variegated granite, without verdure, or gushing rills,
or trace of living thing. They must have appeared like the majestic
corridors of a vast temple, to the inner shrine of which the pillar
of cloud was conducting them by its stately march.

The Red Sea, which must have become like a friend, had been
long ago left behind; and there was no chance of retracing their
path or returning. There was nothing to allure them or arrest their
steps amid the awful desolation and grandeur of those inaccessible
precipices. They would be sometimes almost overwhelmed by the
bare sterility of the scene, and by the awful silence that was stirred
to resent the intrusion of such a multitude upon its ancient reign.
But their course was always onwards; and a deepening awe must
have grown upon their souls, such as became those who were already
treading the precincts of a temple not made with hands, a shrine
of incomparable majesty, to which those vast and sublime avenues
were the befitting approach.

At last it broke on them. After a march of eighteen miles from
the Red Sea, they came out on a perfectly level plain of yellow sand,
some two miles long, and half-a-mile wide, nearly flat, and dotted

over with tamarisk bushes. The mountains which gather around this plain have for the most part sloping sides, and form a kind of natural amphitheatre; but towards the south there is one pile of jagged cliffs which rises sheer upwards in wild precipitousness, whilst behind lies the granite mass of Gebel Mousa, deeply cleft with fissures, and torn, as though it had fought a hard battle with earthquake, storm, and fire. This pile of rocks is called Raṣ Sufsafeh, and was probably "the mount that might be touched and burned with fire." It rises from the plain below as a huge altar; and all that transpired on its summit would have been easily visible to the furthest limits of the camp of two million souls pitched beneath.

Such was the chosen scene for the giving of the Law. There the hosts of Israel remained stationary for long weeks; and there, whilst clouds veiled the heights, and fire played from peak to peak, and mysterious voices, resembling at times a trumpet's notes, awoke unwonted echoes in the heart of the hills, God met with his people and gave them his Law; writing his name, not on tablets of stone merely, but on the entire course of human history.

I. GOD'S OBJECT AT SINAI.—We can but briefly touch on this, as we are most of all concerned with the character of the great leader; but in that more exclusive study we may for a moment consider the impressions which the marvellous scenes associated with Sinai were calculated to produce on the people and on himself.

At the time of the Exodus the world was almost wholly given to idolatry. The first objects of idolatrous worship were probably simply the sun and moon and heavenly bodies, or other conspicuous objects of creative wisdom and power. Afterwards the Deity was supposed to reside in men, and even beasts. Of these, images were made and worshipped—at first covered with drapery, but afterwards in a state of nudity, and exerting the most demoralizing effect. "Professing themselves to be wise, they became fools, and changed the glory of the incorruptible God for the likeness of an image of corruptible man, and of birds, and four-footed beasts, and creeping things. Wherefore God gave them up to the lusts of their hearts" (Rom. i. 22–24, R.V.).

In dealing with this deluge of idolatry, God acted as with the deluge of water that drowned the ancient world. He began with a single family, teaching them the sublime lessons concerning Himself; which when they had perfectly acquired, they were to make the common coin of the world.

Let us notice the successive steps.

First Step.—God chose from the masses of heathendom one man, "called him alone," and led him to follow Him into a strange land. There, shut away from surrounding peoples, He began to teach him about Himself. As a gardener selects one plant that he may bring it to rare perfection, and make it the means of improving the entire sisterhood, so Jehovah spared no time or pains with the first great Hebrew, that being blessed he might be the means of blessing to the race.

Second Step.—God welded the Hebrew people together into one, that they might be able to receive and retain as a part of their national life those great truths with which they were to be entrusted. This welding was accomplished by the tie of common parentage, of which they were justly proud; by the bond of a common occupation, which kept them to themselves as shepherds, apart from the busy traffic of cities and marts of commerce; and, lastly, by the pressure of a common trial, which together with the marvellous deliverance that was granted them, remained fresh and indelible in all after generations, like those colours in the land of their bondage, which in the dry desert air have lasted in unfading vividness for thirty centuries. So perfectly did God do this work, that while other nations have risen, reigned, and fallen, and their disintegration has been utter and final, the children of Abraham endure, like an imperishable rock, undestroyed by the chafe of the waves or the fret of the ages.

Third Step.—God revealed his existence. Into the midst of their bondage tidings came that the god of their fathers was a living God; that He had met one of their number in the desert and had called him by name, and had promised to interfere in their behalf. The news may have excited but a languid interest. They were glad that like other nations of the time they had their tutelary deity, but that was all; and they knew little or nothing beside.

Fourth Step.—God showed by the plagues that He was stronger than the gods of Egypt. Can you not imagine the children of Israel saying, "Our God is great, He has turned the water into blood; but perhaps He is not so strong as Isis, or Osiris, or Serapis, or the sacred bull"? But the wonders which were wrought on the gods of Egypt settled that question for ever.

Fifth Step.—God excited their love and gratitude. You can do anything you like with those you love: but to get, you must give; to excite love, you must declare it. Hence they were touchingly reminded of what He had done: "Ye have seen what I did unto the Egyptians, and how I bare you on eagles' wings, and brought you unto Myself" (Exod. xix. 4).

Sixth Step.—God set Himself to teach them concerning certain of those great qualities, the knowledge of which lay at the foundation of all right dealings between the people and Himself. And in order to achieve his purpose, He made use of outward significant signs; which did more than the most elaborate discourse to instruct the ignorant and sensual people whom He had taken for his own.

Seventh Step.—God clearly designated Moses to be the organ and channel of his communications to man. "Lo, I come unto thee in a thick cloud, that the people may hear when I speak with thee, and believe thee for ever" (ver. 9). It was impossible to forecast the way in which God was fulfilling his purposes at the time; but as we look back on the story we can detect the development of his plan, just as from the summits of the eternal hills we shall see the way by which He has been leading us all the days of our pilgrimage.

II. THE LESSONS OF SINAI.—(1) *The Majesty of God.* The natural scenery was sufficiently majestic; but it became more so as the incidents of the third day were unfolded. Was there not majesty in the thunders and lightnings; in the brooding cloud where clouds were almost unknown; in the flashing lightning dispelling the pitchy gloom; in the trumpet peal echoing through the hills—now soft as a flute rolling through the yielding air, now loud as an organ striking against some outstanding cliff? Meanwhile the clouds dropped water, and there were showers of tropical rain. And it was amid such scenes that God spake. Could any combination of natural phenomena have given grander conceptions of the Majesty of the Divine Nature?

(2) *The Spirituality of God.* What was their God like? Would He assume the form of anything that is in the heaven above, or in the earth beneath, or in the waters under the earth? Would it be in any, or in a combination of all, of these forms that they should see Him who had brought them out of Egypt? But on that memorable occasion, "when Moses brought forth the people out of the camp to meet God,"

they saw no likeness. He was there, for He spoke. But there was no outward form for the eye to discern. It was very hard. The extreme difficulty of the human heart accustoming itself to the worship of what the eye cannot perceive, or the imagination realize, has been attested by the repeated relapse into idolatry, from the days of the golden calf to the crucifix which the Roman Catholic devotee presses to her lips. It has not been easy for mankind to learn this lesson so clearly taught on Sinai, that God is a Spirit.

(3) *The Holiness of God.* This primal lesson was also taught in striking fashion by outward signs which impressed the sense. Bounds were erected to keep the beasts from grazing on the thin herbage of the lower slopes; whoever touched the Mount must die; all clothes were to be carefully washed against that third day; absolute purity was to be observed in heart and life; Moses alone was called up to the top of the Mount, where smoke and fire and lightning flash commingled, and the thunder peal vied with the trumpet-blast; and when he had climbed thither, he was sent all the way down again for the express purpose of charging the people, and even the priests, not to break through upon the Lord to gaze, lest God should break forth upon them. All these significant acts converged to give outward and sensible manifestation of the Holiness of God.

(4) *The Royalty of God.* In their triumphal ode of victory by the shores of the Red Sea, the people had confessed the right of Jehovah to reign over them for ever; but they were yet to learn that He was indeed absolute monarch. The Jewish state as a kingdom, and God was King. And the reality of his government appeared in the way in which Moses himself obeyed his behest. It was a sight never to be forgotten to see how their great leader Moses was absolutely subservient to the command issued from God's pavilion. At the best he was only God's executor, "the passive instrument of the Divine will." The Decalogue was spoken by God Himself "out of the midst of the fire, of the cloud, and of the thick darkness, with a great voice" (Deut. v. 22). Every ordinance of the Law, every custom and provision for domestic and civil life, every item in the construction of the sanctuary and in the ordering of the priests, was due to the direct will of God, spoken from his mouth. "God, and not Moses, was the author of each proviso, the real Legislator, the real Law-giver, the real King; Moses was but the mouthpiece, an intermediary to communicate God's decrees to his people." How clear

was the testimony to the supremacy of the Most High ! Such were some of the lessons taught at Sinai.

III. Moses at Sinai.—He seemed at home there. Though as to his physical system he could not but fear and quake from the unwonted accompaniments of the Divine Glory, yet there was no slavish dread such as would make him draw afar off, as the people did. Mark successive stages in that familiarity between him and God. "Moses went up unto God" (Exod. xix. 3). Having reported God's words to the people, he returned to tell the people's words to the Lord; for we are told "he went down from the mount unto the people" (ver. 14). When Jehovah came down in thunder and smoke, for the third time Moses went up to the top of the mount (ver. 20). When the ten words of the Law had been Spoken, Moses drew near to the thick darkness where God was (Exod. xx. 21). After this, he was bidden to ascend the mountain a fifth time, the elders accompanying him to a certain point, and Joshua still further; but he alone entering the cloud, which was like devouring fire on the top of the mount: and he remained there forty days and forty nights to receive the Divine instructions for the erection of the Tabernacle (Exod. xxiv. 18). A sixth time he returned unto God, offering to be blotted from his book, if only Israel might be spared, and their sin atoned (Exod. xxxii. 32). And yet a seventh time he was invited to come up early in the morning, carrying with him two tablets of stone; and there, as he stood in an alcove of the rocks, the presence of God passed by, and the name of God was proclaimed, and he remained for a second period of forty days and forty nights, descending to the people with shining face, the living evidence of the reality and closeness of the fellowship. "And the Lord spake unto Moses face to face, as a man speaketh unto his friend" (Exod. xxxiii. 11).

This fellowship had an ennobling effect on his character. Not only did his face shine, but his life shone also. There was henceforth a supernatural grace and beauty about his aspect and demeanour which clearly marked him out as "the man of God." His meekness, his gentleness under provocation, his jealousy for the name and cause of God, burnt with an intenser and more even flame.

The life of fellowship with God cannot be built up in a day. It begins with the habitual reference of all to Him, hour by hour, as Moses did in Egypt. But it moves on to more and longer periods of communion. And it finds its consummation and bliss in days and nights of intercession and waiting and holy intercourse. Ah, what patterns are seen on the Mount ! What cries are uttered there ! What visions are seen there ! What revelations are made there ! What injunctions are received there ! Alas for us that we remove so far away from it ! or at the best are admitted to stand only with the elders, and see paved work of sapphire stone beneath God's feet ! Oh for the closer access, the nearer view, the more intimate face to face intercourse, such as is open still to the friends of God !

XVIII

THE VISION OF GOD AND ITS EFFECT

"It came to pass, when Moses came down from Mount Sinai, that he wist not that the skin of his face shone."
—EXOD. xxxiv. 29.

WE ARE justified by the highest authority in deriving spiritual lessons from this incident in the life of the great law-giver. The Apostle expressly refers to it when he says that we all may, with unveiled face, behold the glory of the Lord, and be transformed (2 Cor. iii. 13–18). That blessed vision which of old was given only to the great leader of Israel, is now within reach of each individual believer. The Gospel has no fences to keep off the crowds from the mount of vision; the lowliest and most unworthy of its children may pass upward where the shining glory is to be seen. We are not living in the morning, when the rays of the sun reach only the elect spirits that tower above the rest; but in the noon, when every tiny flower and hidden nook lies in full view of the meridian sun. "We *all* . . . are changed."

I. THE DESIRE TO SEE GOD CARRIES WITH IT THE PLEDGE OF ITS GRATIFICATION. During long years the desire had been growing in the heart of Moses to see the face of God. "Show me now thy way, that I may know Thee"; "I beseech Thee, show me thy glory." Prayers like these were constantly on his lips. And sometimes with him, as with saints of later days, the yearning must have become almost too intense to be borne. No invalid in the dark cold winter days so longs for the summer; no true heart so longs for its mate; no young bride just widowed so longs for the everlasting reunion of heaven, as do some saintly hearts long for God. "Oh that I knew where I might find Him !" "My soul longeth, yea, even fainteth for the courts of the Lord ; my heart and my flesh cry out for the living God." "My soul thirsteth for Thee."

But these longings are certain to be fulfilled, because God is faithful. There is no stronger argument for immortality than this ; it must

121

be, because all men forecast it. There is no stronger argument for
retribution than this; it must be, because men's consciences demand
it. There is no stronger argument for the Being of God than to say,
It must be, because the heart of man craves infinite love; the mind of
man infinite truth; the spirit of man infinite communion with spirit.
And in the same way we must infer, that the very presence of these
intense yearnings for Himself—for face to face fellowship and intercourse—are the herald symptoms, the premonitory signs, that within
our reach there is the possibility of an intercourse with God, which
up till now our hearts have not conceived.

And if we garner every opportunity, cultivate every faculty, and
keep our faces ever towards the mountain of communion, we shall
infallibly find that the heart which yearns for the vision shall not be
left without the vision for which it yearns; and that the yearning is
the unconscious awakening of the soul to the fact that it is standing
on the threshold of the highest privilege possible to man. It is thus
that a babe awakens to a mother's tenderness, and a maiden becomes conscious of the great destiny to which an unexpected love,
which has stolen so mysteriously upon her, beckons. Oh, these
mysterious risings of the water in the river where the barges lie, bearing them up on their arms, rattling their chains, straining their cords,
and bringing them an assurance of the swell and fullness and glory of
the great ocean, which calls to them to launch forth on its broad
expanse and fathomless depths ! "And the Lord said unto Moses, I
will do this thing also that thou hast spoken; for thou hast found grace
in My sight. . . . Be ready in the morning, and come up in the morning unto Mount Sinai."

II. THE GRATIFICATION OF OUR DESIRE DEPENDS ON OUR FULFIL-
MENT OF CERTAIN CONDITIONS.—(1) *We must learn to obey.* This was
the great characteristic of Moses. He was faithful in *all* God's house
as a servant. His proudest title, by which he is known even in
heaven, is "the servant of God." "They sing the song of Moses,
the servant of God" (Rev. xv. 3). And the repeated refrain of the
books of the Pentateuch is the phrase which sounds deep and often,
as the toll of the Inchcape bell over the waves: "as the Lord commanded Moses, so did he." God could always depend on him. He
was a man after his own heart, who could fulfil all his will. And it
was to him, rather than to the disobedient hearts of the people, that
God revealed Himself.

And this is consistent with the words of our Lord, who said, "He that hath my commandments, and keepeth them, he it is that loveth Me; and I will manifest Myself unto him" (John xiv. 21). Clearly, obedience is the stepping-stone to vision. We must be servants ere we can be friends. The path of literal obedience, albeit that it is rough and steep, is the only path to the mountain-summit, with its marvellous revelation. Is it not so always? The discoverer must obey nature, before he can expect to reach the vantage-ground from which to survey the harmony and helpfulness of her mighty laws, and the mystery of her secret processes.

Do not be disobedient to heavenly visions; never turn aside to your own preferences from the narrow path of unswerving loyalty to the voice of God—speaking in his word, and in your heart, and in circumstance. Dare to do right, though you stand alone amongst the recreant hosts; and you will thus fulfil one prime condition of the vision of God.

(2) *We must be willing to pass through the thick cloud.*—"God called to Moses out of the midst of the cloud . . . and Moses went into the midst of the cloud" (Exod. xxiv. 16–18). Thick banks of dense cloud, dark in their earthward aspect, though insufferably bright on their inner side, shut out the light of sun and the spectacles of earth, and shut him in with God. But he had not seen the vision, had he not been willing to pass through the cloud and to stand beneath the shadow of the Divine hand.

The traveller who would pass from the wintry slopes of Switzerland into the summer beauty of the plains of Italy, must be prepared to tunnel the Alps. The garden, the cross, and the grave, are the only way to the Easter morning. The walls must be toned to a neutral tint on which masterpieces of painting are to be exhibited. And it seems indispensable that we should pass into the shadow of bereavement, temptation, and distress, if we are to emerge into God's marvellous light and estimate its brilliance.

> *Not first the light, and after that the dark;*
> *But first the dark, and after that the light.*
> *First, the thick cloud, and then the rainbow arc;*
> *First, the dark grave, and then the resurrection light.*

(3) *We must dare to be alone.*—When we read (Exod. xxxiv. 2, 3) those solemn words, "Be ready in the morning, and come up in the

morning, and present thyself there to Me in the top of the mount: and no man shall come up with thee; neither let any man be seen throughout all the mount, neither let the flocks nor herds feed before the mount"—they seem to echo down to us in other but similar tones, "When thou prayest, enter into thy closet, and when thou hast shut thy door, pray to thy Father which is in secret." Jacob must be left alone if the Angel of God is to whisper in his ear the mystic name of Shiloh; Daniel must be alone if he is to see the celestial vision; John must be banished to Patmos if he is deeply to take and firmly to keep "the print of heaven." The insulated cloud alone contains in its bosom the mighty thunderstorm; that which is stranded on the mountain slope is soon robbed of its electricity.

Valuable as are the prolific opportunities for Christian culture and service which surround us, they will be disastrous indeed in their effect if they rob us of the time that we should otherwise spend with God, or give us a distaste for lonely heart-fellowship. Let the first moments of the day, when the heart is fresh, be given to God. Never see the face of man till you have seen the King. Dare to be much alone on the Mount.

III. WHEN THE CONDITIONS ARE FULFILLED, THE VISION IS SURE.— Perhaps Moses, as he entered the cloud, expected that the Almighty would pass before him, riding upon a cherub, flying upon the wings of the wind, girt with rainbow and storm, while the thunder rolled as drums in his march. But lo! he seemed to stand in a ravine, upon a ledge of rock, shadowed by a hand, whilst through that mountain-rent passed the Divine procession; and a voice, still, sweet, penetrating, told that God was Love.

Mark the progress of revelation to the adoring soul. In Horeb, Moses had stood in the outer court, to learn that God is changeless. In the giving of the Law he had stood in the effulgent glory of the Holy Place, to learn that God is righteous. Now he was admitted to the inner shrine, to learn that the Lord God was merciful and gracious, long-suffering, and abundant in goodness and truth.

The answers to our prayers for spiritual vision may not always come as we expect. But, however they come, come they will. None of those who wait for Him shall be ashamed. He will satisfy desires which He has Himself implanted. The King will be punctual to enter to see the guests who have complied with his conditions.

As to Fletcher of Madeley, to Catherine of Siena, to President Edwards, to Dr. Payson, and to hundreds besides, so to you, when least expecting it, will come the beatific vision, perhaps constraining you to cry, as John Tennant did: "Hold, Lord, it is enough! or the frail vessel will break beneath the weight of glory."

IV. SUCH VISIONS LEAVE UNMISTAKABLE TRACES.—The face of Moses shone: and did not his heart and life shine also? Could it have been otherwise? Linen in which the housewife has laid rosemary and lavender will smell fragrantly; ordinary iron placed near a magnet becomes magnetic; those that are in king's courts catch a refined and courteous mien; the friend of wise men gets wisdom; the members of a closely-knit family contract by association some tiny gesture, a peculiarity which betrays their oneness; it is proverbial how on t᾿ e faces of an aged couple there is seen a strong resemblance, so that each reflects the other. And it is impossible for us to be much with God without becoming godly, *i.e.*, God-like.

The old legends of ᾿he saints tell of those who, by long meditation on the crucifixion of the Lord, received in their very flesh the marks of his wounds. There is certainly a spiritual counterpart of this in the long, fixed gaze of the soul on the vision of God, by which the lineaments of the Divine beauty pass into the life, and light it up with a loveliness which is not of earth.

V. SUCH TRACES ARE NOT PERCEIVED BY THOSE WHO PRESENT THEM.—"Moses wist not that his face shone." He was glorious in all eyes but his own.

There is a law known to medical men as Holland's law; which affirms that whenever attention is directed specially to any one organ of the body, the action of that organ is more or less disturbed. If, for instance, we begin to think of our heart, counting its beats, and listening to its throbs, we disturb its rhythmic action. There are few who can let the physician feel their pulse with perfect composure; and he is generally obliged to make some allowance for the effects of this self-consciousness. So with the functions of digestion, and respiration, and thought. These great and vital processes of the body go on most healthily and satisfactorily, when they are not made direct subjects of attention. And in these respects we may trace a close analogy between the physical and the spiritual life of man. A counterpart of Holland's law pervades the physiology of the spiritual life. We shall do best, and make quickest progress, when we know it not.

True Christian excellence is as unconscious of its beauty as Moses was; whenever it becomes self-conscious it loses its charm. Beware of the man who talks about his graces. There is such a thing as being proud of humility, and making capital out of our nothingness. The man who boasts of a shining face is a counterfeit and a cheat. The possessor of the genuine article never talks about it, never thinks about it; and would be almost overwhelmed to hear of any such thing being ascribed to him. The charm of a little child is its utter unconsciousness of self; and that is the charm in true God-likeness. It is like the bloom on a peach, the dew-jewels on the morning lawn, or the stillness of the surface of a mountain pool.

XIX

THE BROKEN SENTENCE

"Yet now, if Thou wilt forgive their sin——; and if not, blot me, I
pray Thee, out of Thy book which Thou hast written."
—Exod. xxxii. 32.

THIS is one of the most pathetic verses of the Bible, which bears on
its face the evidence of its genuineness. It could not have emanated
from the mind or pen of some later scribe; because so entirely
unexpected, so strange, and yet so likely. It reminds us of the shaft
of a graceful column broken off in the middle; or of a strain of
plaintive music hushed to sudden silence by the snapping of a
string. It is the fragment of a sentence of which we would have
given much to hear the conclusion; but who can presume to finish
that which in this supreme hour was choked by a paroxysm of
grief, a sob of irrepressible emotion?

I. THE PROBLEM WITH WHICH HE HAD TO DEAL. (1) *Their idolatry.*
—After the utterance of the ten great words of Sinai, the people,
frightened by the thunderings and lightnings, and the voice of the
trumpet, and the smoke of the mountain, entreated Moses to act
as their daysman and mediator. "They said unto him: Speak thou
with us, and we will hear; but let not God speak with us, lest we
die" (Exod. xx. 19). The great lawgiver and leader, acting on their
request, thereupon withdrew himself into the divine pavilion, and
was absent for about six weeks.

After the return of the seventy elders who had accompanied
Moses to some lower ledge of the mountain but had returned without him, the people were doubtless well content. Better to be
temporarily deprived of their leader, than be exposed to those
terrible thunderings. But, after awhile, they became uneasy and rest-
less. From one to another the word passed, "Where is he? He did not
take food enough with him to sustain him for so long. Has he met

with some mishap on those lonely steeps ? or perchance he has been destroyed by that burning fire, or absorbed into the unseen." "As for this Moses, the man that brought us up out of the land of Egypt, we wot not what is become of him " (Exod. xxxii. 1). And then turning to Aaron, the man of words, sure that neither he nor twenty like him could fill the gap which the loss of Moses had caused, they cried, "Up, make us gods, which shall go before us."

We may notice, as we pass, the essential nature of idolatry. For in this marvellous chapter we have its entire history, from the first cry of the soul, which betrays so marvellous a yearning for an idol, to the draining of the last bitter dregs, with which, when ground to powder, the idolater has to drink its very dust. Men sometimes speak of idolaters bowing down before material forms, whether of gold, stone, or wood, as if they supposed that these were Divine, and possessed Divine attributes—and such may be the case with the more degraded and debased; but in the beginning it was not so. And if we carefully study the question in all its bearings, we shall discover that the idolater does not—in the first instance, at least— look upon his image as God, but as a representation or manifestation of God. It is an attempt on the part of the human spirit, which shrinks from the effort of communion with the unseen and spiritual, to associate God with what it can own and handle; so as to have a constant and evident token of the presence and favour of God.

This was the case of Israel. It was only three months since they had stood by the Red Sea, and seen its waters roll in pride over the hosts of Pharaoh. Every day since then God's love had followed them. For them the heaven had given bread, and the rocks had flowed with water; and his cloud had sailed majestically through the sky, shielding them in the daylight, and burning like a watch-fire through the night. And even at the time with which we are dealing the whole summit of the mount was crowned by the pavilion of cloud, which was the emblem of his presence in their midst. But notwithstanding all, they were carried away before that imperious craving of the human heart, which cries out for a sensible image for its worship.

Their idolatry, then, was a violation, not of the first, but of the second commandment. They did not propose to renounce Jehovah— that was left for the days of Ahab; but they desired to worship Jehovah under the form of a calf, and in distinct violation of the emphatic prohibition, which said, "Thou shalt not make unto thee any graven image, or any likeness of any thing that is in heaven above, or that is in the earth beneath; thou shalt not bow down thyself to them, nor serve them." This was the sin also of Jeroboam.

(2) *Their Degradation.*—There can be no doubt that the worship of the calf was accompanied with the licentious orgies which were a recognised part of Egyptiah idolatry. As much as this is implied in the narrative. "The people sat down to eat and to drink, and rose up to play." In the R.V. a striking emendation is given of the 25th verse. "Moses saw that the people were broken loose; for Aaron had let them loose for a derision among their enemies." And from this we may infer that the bonds of continence, that had restrained them since the Exodus, had been suddenly slackened; with the result of their breaking from all restraint, and giving themselves up to their unholy riot.

(3) *The Claims of God.*—There was every reason to believe that God would exact the full amount of penalty; not because He was vindictive, but because the maintenance of his authority seemed to demand it. The righteousness of his character, the inviolability of his oath, the authority of the Ten Commandments, so recently given, combined to make it necessary that He should do as He had said.

And yet, on the other hand, there was the fear lest, if, to use the language of men, God's anger waxed hot and He consumed them, the Egyptians might say, "For evil did He bring them forth to slay them on the mountains, and to consume them from the face of the earth." And thus Jehovah's character might be misunderstood and maligned amongst the nations around.

How could God maintain his character with his own people without imperilling it with the Egyptians ? If he spared the people, they would begin to think that neither his threats nor his promises were worth their heed. And if He destroyed them, his glory would be dimmed; and He might seem to have become unmindful of the oath which He swore by Himself to his servants, Abraham, Isaac, and Israel, that He would multiply their seed, and give the land of Canaan to them as an heritage for ever. So greatly did these considerations weigh with Moses, that he refused the Divine offer to make him the only survivor of the host, and the progenitor of a great nation.

It would almost seem as if this proposal resembled the suggestion made to Abraham, that he should offer up his only son, Isaac.

In each case God tried—or tested—his servant. But there is this great difference between the temptations of the devil and of God. The former seeks to bring out all the evil, and to make it permanent, as the streams of lava poured from the heart of a volcano: the latter seeks to bring out all the good, and to make it ours; for moral qualities never become ours till we have put them into practice.

II. THE EMOTIONS WITH WHICH HIS SOUL WAS STIRRED.—In the mount he acted as intercessor. When God told him all that was transpiring in the plain below, and showed the glittering sword of justice suspended over the guilty nation by a thread, he pleaded for the people whom he loved. "And Moses besought the Lord his God. . . . Turn from thy fierce wrath, and repent of this evil against thy people." "And the Lord repented of the evil which He thought to do unto his people."

On his way down from the mount, when he came near enough to see the calf and the dancing, peering over some over-hanging ledge of rock, the old impetuous vehemence which had characterized him in earlier life, and had slept for so many years, broke out with all its early intensity. It was not against the people, but against their sin, that his anger flamed out. "Moses' anger waxed hot; and he cast the tables out of his hands, and brake them beneath the mount." Those splintered bits leaping from crag to crag are an apt symbol of the inability of man, even the holiest, to keep intact the holy Law of God.

When he reached the camp, he seems to have strode into the astonished throng, broken up their revelry, and overturned their calf, ordering it to be destroyed, and the fragments mingled with the water they drank. But as this did not avail to stay the inveterate evil, he was compelled to use more drastic measures, and by the sword of Levi to extinguish it with the life-blood of three thousand men.

Then when the next day came, when the camp was filled with mourning over those newly-made graves, when the awful reaction had set in on the people and himself, the tide seems to have turned. His indignation was succeeded by bitter sorrow and pity. The thunderstorm was broken into floods of tears. The pitiable state to which their sin had reduced them aroused his deepest compassion; and he said unto the people, "Ye have sinned a great sin: and now I will go up unto the Lord, peradventure I shall make an atonement for your sin" (ver. 30); but he did not tell them the purpose which was in his heart, nor the price which he was purposing to pay.

III. THE OFFER THAT HE MADE.—He went quietly and thoughtfully back to the presence-chamber of God, as the people stood beholding. "Peradventure," he had said—he was not sure. He felt that the sin was very great. He could not see how God could go back from his solemn threatenings. He was convinced that if the merited judgments were averted, it must be in consequence of an atonement. Yet, what atonement could there be? Animals could not avail, though they were offered in hecatombs. There was only one thing he could suggest—he could offer himself. He was, of course, by no means clear that even this would be accepted or avail; but he could at least make the offer. This was the secret which he locked in his breast as he climbed the mountain. And it was this which made him say. "Peradventure." He could not be sure that the ransom price would be large enough.

It may be asked how he came to think of atonement. But we must remember that probably there had already been much talk between God and himself about the sacrifices which the people were to offer. Again and again had the word *atonement* been employed: he had learned that one by suffering could redeem others; he had seen the deep possibilities in the law of substitution; and it seemed a natural thing, therefore, to purpose that he, the chosen servant, the prince and leader of the people, should be weighed in the scale against the nation, and God should accept his blood as a ransom for their life.

And Moses confessed his people's sin to God, and added: "Yet now, if Thou wilt forgive their sin——". He would not finish that sentence. He could not trust himself to depict the blessed consequences that would ensue, if only God would forgive. If Thou wilt forgive, freely, and without a ransom price, *then* thy noblest attributes will appear; *then* my tongue shall sing aloud of thy goodness; *then* I will bind myself to thy service with new enthusiasm; *then* the people surely will become touched with the passion of gratitude and love.

But the dark fear oppressed him that free pardon was too much to expect. Ah, how little did he realize the love of God in Jesus Christ our Lord! And he therefore added: "And if not, blot me, I pray Thee, out of thy book which Thou hast written." That book may be the Book of Life; or it may be the registry of God's people, whether in this life or in the next. So that the proposal was either that he should there and then die, and not see the good land beyond Jordan; or that he should cease to be numbered with God's people, and miss for ever the beautiful vision, finding his portion among the reprobate.

This proposal was made deliberately and thoughtfully. He had had ample time to think it over during the long and tedious climb from the mountain foot. He was quite prepared for God to accept it. He would have counted himself highly honoured to have been allowed to be a sin-offering on those heights. Oh, how the heart of God must have moved towards the faithful servant, whose proposal recalled another scene in the far-away ages of eternity, when the Son of God undertook to redeem man by making an atonement through the shedding of his own blood !

Of course, the offer was not accepted. No one can atone for his own sin, much less for the sins of others. Yet the people were spared. The passing by of their transgression was rendered possible by the propitiation which was to be offered in the course of the ages on the cross (Rom. iii. 25). And though they were threatened with the loss of the Divine presence in its richer manifestations, yet the Angel of God was sent before them to lead them into the land of promise.

XX

GOD'S PRESENCE OUR REST

" My presence shall go with thee, and I will give you rest."
—EXOD. xxxiii. 14.

THIS assurance of rest is as applicable to the present age as to that of the Exodus. Nay, perhaps there is a special message in it to these feverish days, so filled with discord, confusion, and strife. Its very utterance shows a deep acquaintance with the heart of man. For there is a settled conviction with us all that we are not to live ever thus, the victims of merciless disquiet.

Every revolution—the Anarchist's plot and the Socialist's dream, the well-meant effort to bring about the kingdom of heaven by social reconstruction—is a plea on the part of men for rest. But that rest must be sought deeper down than in circumstances. It must begin at the centre of our being, and in its accord with the being of God. His presence must be welcome to us, and accompany us, or rest is a vain dream.

I. THE CIRCUMSTANCES BY WHICH THIS ASSURANCE WAS CALLED FORTH.—(1) Moses was a very lonely man. Perhaps more lonely in the midst of the two millions of people whom he was leading as a flock, than he had been amid the solitudes of the desert, tending the flock of Jethro. The very contrast between his lofty enjoyment of Divine communion, and the people, always set on sensual pleasure, must have lent intensity to the isolation of his spirit, which reared itself amid their sensual longings, as the peak of Sufsafeh above the lower ranges of Sinai. "And Moses said unto the Lord, see, Thou sayest unto me, bring up this people; and Thou hast not let me know whom Thou wilt send with me." What a sigh there is here for companionship!

It is certain that these words will be read by many whose lives are outwardly solitary. Some are left during long hours to bear the burden of the home, or of suffering, or of foreign service, like a sentry on night-duty at a lone post. Others amid crowds are not less solitary; many soldiers, but no brother-officer; many voices, but the one voice missing; many companions, but no friend. In the physical world we are told that in the most solid bodies the atoms do not touch; and how often though the crowd throngs us we are not conscious that any one has touched us. It is to that state of mind that the assurance of the text was given.

(2) In addition to this, the hosts were soon to leave the mountain region of Sinai, with which Moses had been familiar during his shepherd life, in order to take the onward road through unknown deserts, infested by daring and experienced foes. What though the pillar and cloud led them slowly along those solemn desert pathways, and at night shed a broad flood of light on the clustered tents of the desert encampment; yet the prospect of that journey through the great and terrible wilderness was sufficient to appal the stoutest heart.

Such a summons to arise and depart is often sounding with its bugle-call in our ears. We are not like those who travel by the metal track of the railroad, on which they have been to and fro every day for years, and are able to tell exactly the names and order of the stations; but like an exploring expedition in an absolutely unknown district, when even the leader, as he leaves his hammock in the morning, does not know where it will be slung at night. What seems a monotonous life, always the same, does not revolve around a beaten circle, as the horse or ass winding up buckets from a well; but is ever striking out over new tracts of territory, which we have not traversed before.

(3) Still further difficulties had lately arisen in connection with the people's transgression. From a careful study of the passage it would seem that a change was proposed by their Almighty Friend. Hitherto He had gone in the midst of them. Now He avowed his intention of substituting an angel for Himself, lest He should suddenly consume the people because of their stiff-neckedness (ver. 3). Already the people had been bidden to strip themselves of their ornaments; and the tent, which was recognised as the temporary pavilion for God, must be pitched without the camp, afar off from the camp, so that those who sought the Lord were compelled to take a considerable journey to reach his visible shrine. But now it seemed likely that some sensible diminution of the evidence of the Divine presence and favour was about to take place; and the fear of this stirred the soul of the

great leader to its depths. Like Jacob at the fords of the Jabbok, he felt that he could not let God go, and he told Him so: "If thy presence go not with us, carry us not up hence." Better abandon thy mighty scheme, slay us at once, and wrap us in a winding sheet of sand, than allow us to take another step without thy presence.

Are there not times with many of us when we have reason to fear that, in consequence of some sad failure or sin on our part, the Lord may be obliged to withdraw the conscious enjoyment of his love? A chill fear lays its icy hand upon the strings of our heart, and almost petrifies it into silence. "Supposing He should be compelled to leave me to myself, to withdraw his tender mercies, to shut up his compassions. Supposing that I should be like a sledge abandoned in Arctic snows, or a ship abandoned by its crew in mid-ocean. Supposing that the fate of Saul should be mine, and that of me God should say, It repenteth me that I have made him king." Such thoughts quicken the pace of the soul as it goes to his footstool.

II.—THE PLACE WHERE THIS ASSURANCE WAS GIVEN.—The earlier intercourse between the servant, "faithful in all his house," and Him who had appointed him, seems to have been on the mountain summit. But after the outburst of the people's sin, a change was made which did not necessitate such prolonged or distant absences from the camp. Indeed, he was absent for only one other period of forty days (chap. xxxiv. 28) till the time of his death, some thirty-eight years afterwards.

During the prolonged interview which he had been permitted to enjoy, God had spoken to him much of the Tabernacle which was shortly to be reared. He at once saw the blessedness of this proximity of the shrine for worship and fellowship, and his ardent soul seems to have been unable to brook delay. A tent was therefore selected; it may have been his own, or one specially prepared, and was pitched "without the camp, afar off from the camp. And he called it the Tent of Meeting; and it came to pass that every one which sought the Lord went out into the tent of meeting, which was without the camp" (ver. 7, R.V.).

But its special benefit was obvious in the case of Moses himself. It was no longer necessary for him to climb to the mountain summit, entrusted with errands on behalf of the people, or eager for advice in difficult problems. He was able to transact all necessary business by going out to the tent. And when it was rumoured through the camp that he was about to do so, "all the people rose up" to see the marvellous spectacle, "and stood, every man at his tent door," looking after him; because, so soon as he entered into the tent, the pillar of cloud descended from its position in mid-heaven, and stood at the door of the tent, the vehicle and emblem of the Divine presence. Thus "the Lord spake unto Moses face to face, as a man speaketh unto his friend"; and Moses spake to his Father, who is in secret, with the freedom of a child. And as the people beheld that wondrous sight of God stooping to commune with man, they "rose up and worshipped, every man in his tent door" (ver. 10).

It was there that this amazing colloquy took place. Moses spoke of his loneliness, and asked who was to be associated with him in his great task; and contrasted this silence on the part of God in a particular which so closely concerned his comfort and efficiency with all his other dealings with him. "Yet Thou hast said, I know thee by name, and thou hast also found grace in my sight" (ver. 12). Then it seemed as if that faithful heart suddenly caught sight of a blessing more transcendent in glory than any he had yet dared to ask. His petition was couched in great humility, sandwiched between a double reference to the grace to which he owed everything; but he ventured to suggest that God should Himself show him his ways, that he might know Him. It was as if he said, Wilt Thou Thyself be my comrade and companion—my referee in difficulty; my adviser in perplexity; my friend in solitude? Thine angels are strong and fair and good; but none of them will suffice me, nothing short of Thyself. Without Thee, it were better for me to relinquish my task and die; but with Thee, no difficulty can baffle, no fear alarm, no obstacle deter.

And God's answer came back on his spirit with music and balm, "My presence shall go with thee, and I will give thee rest" (ver. 14). Nothing was said as to the people. The promise of the Divine presence was made apparently to Moses alone.

But faith gets bolder as it mounts. Each answer to its claims makes it claim more. We may seriously question whether our faith is of the right quality if it is unable to compass more in its hand to-day than it did a year ago. And, therefore, Moses not only took the assurance of the Divine presence for himself, but asked that it should be extended to include the people. "Wherein shall it be known here that I and thy people have found grace in thy sight? Is it not in that Thou goest with us? so shall we be separated, I and thy people, from all the people that are upon the face of the earth" (ver. 16).

In this request also he was successful. "And the Lord said unto Moses, I will do this thing also that thou has spoken; for thou hast found grace in my sight" (ver. 17). There are moments of holy intercourse with God, rapturous, golden moments, in the lives of all his servants; when next they visit us, and we would make the most of their brief, bright, rapturous glow, let us plead, not only for ourselves, but for others, asking for them an equal blessedness.

III. THE BLESSEDNESS WHICH THIS ASSURANCE GUARANTEED.— There was, first, the Divine presence; and there was, secondly, the promised Rest—not the rest of Canaan, for this Moses never saw; but a deeper and more blessed inheritance, which may be the portion of all faithful souls. But at their heart these two are one. The Divine presence is Rest.

Of course, the conscious presence of God with us is only possible on three conditions.

Firstly, we must walk in the light, as He is in the light; for He will have no fellowship with the unfruitful works of darkness, or turn aside to go with us on any crooked path of our own choosing.

Secondly, we must recognise that the blood of Jesus Christ his Son constantly cleanseth us from all sin; not only that which we judge and confess, but that also which is only seen by his pure and holy eyes.

Thirdly, we must claim the gracious aid of the Holy Spirit, to make real that presence, which is too subtle for the eye of man, unless it be specially enlightened.

And above all, we must remember that for us, at least, that presence is localized in the man Christ Jesus. For us there is no attenuated mist of presence, though a mist of light; but a Person in whom that presence is made real and touches us. But when these conditions are fulfilled, the blessed soul enters upon an experience of the presence of God which can find no better words to express its bliss than the psalmist's, as he turned from the prosperity of the wicked to consider his own estate: "Nevertheless, I am continually with Thee; Thou has holden me by my right hand . . . Whom have I in heaven but Thee ? and there is none upon earth that I desire beside Thee" (Psa. lxiii. 23, 25).

And the sense of that presence is Rest. I have a vision of a woodland glade. A group of tired, frightened children are cowering around the bole of an old tree, dropping the fragile, withered flowers from their hands and pinafores, as the first great drops of the thunder shower, which had been darkening the sky, begin to fall. They have lost their way; they sob bitterly, and crowd together. Suddenly through the wood there comes a quick step, beneath which the twigs crackle and break—Father has come, and as he carries some in his strong arms through the storm on the nearest track for home, and the others run at his side, they have learnt that there is a presence which is Rest.

XXI

TABERNACLE BUILDING

"According to all that I shew thee, even so shall ye make it . . . after the pattern which was showed thee in the mount."

—EXOD. xxv. 9, 40.

THE HEART of the Jewish people was the Tabernacle, around which their tents circled, and the movements of which determined the journeyings of the host. The Tabernacle also taught them some of the deepest thoughts about God, in a kind of picture language, which was best suited to their immature minds. These we can touch on but incidentally, as our main point is the part borne by Moses in its creation.

We must remember that the children of Israel did not possess a language like our own, with many words, and a rich vocabulary, capable of expressing all kinds of abstract ideas, such as love, wisdom, purity, spirituality, holiness. We hardly realize how great a hindrance to the communication of spiritual truth arises from the lack of suitable words to act as the channels of thought. How could you speak of love to savages, if the only word for it in their language had impure and coarse associations? So that before making his revelation God had to provide language for his thoughts. This He did largely in the construction of the Tabernacle.

I. THE CONCEPTION OF THE TABERNACLE.—The pattern in the mount! Then clearly there must have been some visible phenomenon, some bright apparition, some glorious picture cast on the clouds or built on the old rocks. There may have been stakes and curtains, cherubs and lamps, gold and silver, altar and candlestick; but they would not bear the touch—they existed as a beautiful dream, like some mystery of cloud that stands for a moment in the heavens at sunset, and then is gone.

But it is almost inconceivable that God did not at the same time explain to Moses those wonderful conceptions of his own nature, and

139

his relations to men, which were intended to be set forth in this material structure. In those days of hallowed intercourse, the Almighty Teacher must have impressed on the reverent and receptive mind of his pupil trains of holy thought which engrossed and delighted him. It may be that even to him they were first conveyed under those pictorial forms in which they were afterwards presented to the people; but in any case they were surely communicated by the Spirit which reveals the deep things of God, and makes them known to those who love Him. They were as follows:—

God's willingness to share man's life.—If the people had only seen the devouring fire on the top of Sinai, the pavilion of God's presence, they would never have dared to think that there was any community of interest between Him and them. To their minds, He would always have seemed distant and unapproachable. So God said, "Let them make Me a sanctuary, that I may dwell among them" (ver. 8); and He promised concerning it, "I will dwell among the children of Israel, and will be their God" (Exod. xxix. 45).

Thus it was ordained that this larger tent should be pitched among them, only differing from their own in its proportions and materials; but standing on the same level sand, struck and pitched at the same hour with theirs, and enduring the same vicissitudes of weather and travel. Did not this say, as plainly as words could, that the tabernacle of God was with men, and that He was willing to dwell with them and become their God? Did it not teach that Jehovah had become a pilgrim with the pilgrim host; no longer a God afar off, but a sharer in their national fortunes? And is not this the very lesson of the Incarnation? May we not venture to suppose that the Church, that holy body which being prepared for the Son of God, was even then revealed to the faithful servant? and that in his wonderful structure he was taught to repeat, in material forms, that mystic union of spirit, soul, and body, in the man Christ Jesus, of which the holy of holies, the holy place, the outer court were the transient but striking emblem?

It was thus that the mind of man was prepared to learn that God could become flesh, and tabernacle amongst us. It was thus that the first syllables were coined which were to be built up into the name Emmanuel. It was thus that the Incarnation was prefigured. For the body of Jesus is the true Tabernacle, which the Lord hath pitched, and not man; that body which was born of the pure Virgin, in which He abode with men, and through which He achieved redemption.

The Greatness of God.—To this, too, a visible expression was to be given. The Tabernacle was the most superb building of its kind ever reared by man. It must have cost at least a quarter of a million sterling—an immense sum for that fugitive nation of slaves. The silver pedestals placed at intervals along the sand to hold the upright boards; the gorgeous tapestry which composed ceiling and walls; the golden furniture, of which the seven-branched candelabra alone weighed one hundredweight of gold, equal to £5,500 in value; the brass wrought into sixty brazen pillars, with their silver capitals and hooks, from which were suspended curtains of so slight a gauze that people could see all that was transpiring in the outer court. How costly were these !

On that new year's day, the anniversary of the Exodus (Exod.xl.17), as it stood forth completed in the desert sunshine, it must have seemed to all who beheld it as fair as the New Jerusalem did to the eye of the seer, when he beheld it descending out of heaven from God; and must have furnished new and enlarged conceptions of the Divine majesty: though to the eye of Moses there must have been almost a disappointment, because the actual fell so far short of the pattern he had seen.

God's Unity.—All around, the nations were under the spell of idolatry. But the Tabernacle, with all its differing parts, and materials, and accessories, was one. One ark; one incense altar; one altar of burnt-offering; one sacred purpose in every order and rite for the putting away of uncleanness. It stood, therefore, among men as a perpetual protest against idolatry, and as an emphatic witness to the Unity of God. "Hear, O Israel; the Lord our God is one Lord." Such was the perpetual message that floated on the desert air from that unique structure.

But how sublime, how awe-inspiring must that message have been, as it first broke on the heart of Moses ! He knew it before, but he saw it as one who looks into the heart of truth; comparing small things with great, it was as when we look into the eye of our friend, and detect there depths of life and love which we could not put into words, and which had passed our thoughts.

God's Spirituality.—On the mountain the lawgiver saw the robes of the King, but not the King; his glory, but not his person; his back part, but not his face; and the conception that God was a Spirit was conveyed to the people in that most striking form.

Enter the holy place; your eye is arrested by the heavy but magnificent curtain, wrought with cherubim, that cuts off six feet of the length of the entire structure. Pull that aside, and you pass into a chamber which is a perfect cube, a miniature of the New Jerusalem, whose length, and breadth, and height, are equal. In the Egyptian temple, this apartment would contain the crocodile or ibis; but here there was only a box, over which forms of exquisite beauty bent with outspread wings, and between them a light shone which was not borrowed from sun or stars. Could anything more significantly convey the idea that God was a Spirit?

This absence of any visible form in the inner shrine most astonished the rough soldier Pompey, who strode with eager curiosity across the floor, which had never before been pressed by aught but the unsandalled foot of the high priest once a year. He expected to find some visible embodiment of Jehovah, and turned contemptuously away deriding the empty void. But to Moses it must have been an unparalleled conception, overpowering his thoughts.

God's Purity.—The impression of this was produced by a series of comparisons. First, the Tabernacle stood within a courtyard fenced from public approach, the outer part could be trodden only by those men who had passed through certain rites of purification; and as to the inner, it could only be trodden once a year by the high priest, carefully cleansed by many rites, and clad in garments of special design, whilst the blood of slain animals, selected out of the herds for their freedom from any blemish or speck, was sprinkled around. All was done to impress upon the people the care with which they must approach God; and in this way impressions of his holiness were wrought into the national mind, which succeeding centuries have not been able to efface.

And throughout these arrangements, and notably by these repeated references to the blood of sacrifices that was to be shed and sprinkled, Moses became much familiarized with the philosophy of the Atonement. He must have seen across the centuries the cross of Jesus, with its mystery of love and sacrifice and substitution for the sins of men; and there must have arisen a very clear prevision of those various aspects of that marvellous death, which were faintly shadowed forth in the offerings, and which touch God and the believer, the offender in ignorance, and the sinner in presumption, the great world of men, and apparently the universe of God.

Such thoughts as these must have penetrated the soul of Moses as he waited before God, oblivious to the flight of time, the waning love and idolatry of his people, or the demands of the body for food.

And as we behold the great spectacle of that rapt and spell-bound soul, we get some conception of one part at least of the engagements of eternity, and we are stirred to seek after a more intimate knowledge of God.

Oh to know God ! Not to know *about* Him, but to know Him; to "follow on to know the Lord"; to think his thoughts; to give Him time to convey his thoughts into our minds; to acquaint ourselves with Him, who, indeed, invites us to the knowledge, and sets open all the doors of his nature for us to enter. This were better than all beside; no rapturous experience, no deliverance from evil, no flight of emotion, could so repay our soul as this, which must carry in its embrace all of these. It were well, indeed, to suffer the loss of all things to know Him !

II. THE REPRODUCTION OF THE PATTERN.—There is a special interest to us all in this. We are not called to build again the Tabernacle, after that old pattern which has served its purpose, and fallen into disuse because superseded by the clearer revelations of the Gospel; yet there is an analogy which is full of instruction and inspiration in the life of every true believer, and deserves our attention for a moment.

As the Tabernacle dwelt in the mind of God before it was reproduced on the desert sands, so does the life of each one exist, as a conception of that same infinite intelligence—which comprehends in its sweep the flight of an angel with the everlasting Gospel, and the fall of a sparrow to the ground.

When a child is born into the world, with all its faculties shut up within it, as a flower in the bud, there is in the mind of God a perfect picture of what that life may become, an ideal to which it may be conformed. There is a clear anticipation of what it will be; but side by side there is a distinct prevision of what it might be. And if only that pattern could be seen and literally reproduced, if only that life could attain to the Divine ideal, there would be no room for regret or disappointment. It would fulfil its complete purpose as a thought of the Divine mind, and attain its perfect consummation and bliss.

So with the believer standing on the threshold of the Christian life, full of hope and purpose. For him also there is a perfect ideal stored in the Divine nature, of a life full of the blessedness of the Beatitudes, and overflowing with the mighty works of the Gospels.

If only it were realized from day to day !—of growing glory, from strength to strength, from grace to grace. Alas, that with so many of us, as the years have passed, we have wrought our own evil will and followed our own design !

The main inquiry for us all as we enter on any fresh enterprise, or even pass over the threshold of each new day, should be, *not* How would other men act ? *nor* What will make for my own advantage ? *nor* What would increase my reputation, or add to my gains ? but—What is God's ideal, God's thought, God's pattern? And our one aim should be to understand it, sure that to fulfil it is to have lived well.

God's Pattern was Comprehensive.—No tassel, nor socket, nor tiny detail, was left to the fancy or ingenuity of the artificers ; all was comprehended in the Divine pattern. Of every detail God had a plan ; because in each some purpose was hidden, and the symmetry of the whole depended on the perfection of each part. So in life God's thought covers all details. Nothing is too trivial to be made a matter of prayer and supplication. No great life is possible that does not comprehend in its scheme and scope attention to the commonplaces and trifles of character.

God's Plan was unfolded gradually.—Probably the account of the revelation of the successive parts of the Tabernacle is an exact transcript of the method by which the Divine design was unfolded to Moses' thought. Line upon line, precept upon precept—such is ever the Divine method. If we may so put it, the plan of the life of Jesus was only unfolded to his human intelligence a step at a time. Remember how He said, "the Son can do nothing of Himself, but what He seeth the Father do." "He will show Him greater works than these." The eye of the perfect Servant was always fixed on the development of his Father's scheme for Him ; this was shown in the touch of a wasted hand, the cry of an agonized parent, the pressure of the hate of his foes, the demands of the crowds.

We shall not be able to see far in front, nor the whole completed plan of our life ; but as we complete one thing, another will be revealed, and then the next and the next. It may be that we shall have to fulfil the different portions of the Tabernacle of our life, without apparent connection with each other, "by divers portions and in divers manners," and we shall not understand the Divine purpose ; but at the end of life we shall see that it was one complete and exquisite structure, of which no part was wanting.

God's Plan was commensurate with the people's resources.—As the pattern was there on the Mount, there were the materials for its realization in the possession of the people below—the gold and silver and precious stones; the blue and purple and scarlet; the fine linen and goats' hair; the rams' skins and badgers' skins; the genius of the artificers; and the willingness of the people.

God never gives a man a pattern without making Himself responsible for the provision of all materials needed for its execution. Take God's plan, and then trust God utterly for the needful grace; it is there; it only awaits the claim of your faith. All things are added to the man who seeks first and only the kingdom of God. If the materials are not forthcoming, you may seriously question whether you are not working on a plan of your own. God will not provide for a single tassel of your own addition to his scheme.

God's Plan must be resolutely Obeyed.—Again and again in the last chapter of Exodus we are told that all was done, "as the Lord commanded Moses." This was his supreme joy and satisfaction, that he had not added to or diminished from the Divine command; and so the work was finished. It would be well for us to cultivate the habit of immediate and entire subservience to the prompting of the Divine will, repeating it in the tiniest details as well as in the most difficult experiences.

Thus would the human life become harmonious with the Divine, the tabernacles of our lives would become the home of Him that inhabiteth eternity, and whose name is Holy; and there would be the settling down upon us of the Divine Shekinah, "the cloud by day and fire by night," through all our journeys, till we reach our Father's home.

God's Plan is always Progressive.—In pursuing the earlier stages of the Divine tuition, Moses was specially occupied with elaborating the elementary idea of sacrifice, as in the case of the Paschal Lamb. The next stage was the building of the Tabernacle, with which we have now been engaged. But this was not the final form of the Divine revelation to which he was called to give visible shape. In after years, when disease was mowing down thousands of victims throughout the camp, as a judgment on the murmurings of the people, their leader was summoned to make a serpent of brass, and place it on a pole, that all who looked might live.

In that supreme moment, he caught sight of the dying Lord, and discerned, not only the fact, but the method of his death. To no other Old Testament seer, so far as we can learn, was it given to know that Jesus must be lifted up upon a cross. But this was permitted to him who had faithfully wrought out the Divine plan in its earlier stages; and he, too, was privileged to set forth, so graphically and simply, the nature of saving faith. "As Moses lifted up the serpent in the wilderness, so must the Son of Man be lifted up, that whosoever believeth in Him should not perish, but have everlasting life."

Thus is it always. As we climb the hill, the horizon expands; as we do God's will more thoroughly, we know his doctrine more completely; as we follow the Divine plan, we are permitted to look into and proclaim those deeper things, "which God hath prepared for them that love Him."

XXII

THE START FROM SINAI

"And Moses said unto Hobab, We are journeying unto the place of which the Lord said, I will give it you. Come thou with us, and we will do thee good."

—NUM. x. 29.

ISRAEL sojourned under the shadow of Sinai for about eleven months —long enough to see the round of the seasons; but the green verdure of the spring and the fading tints of the autumn would leave no trace on the appearance of those vast sandstone rocks. But what a change had been wrought in their condition! They arrived there a fugitive and unorganized people: they left it a mighty nation in battle array, provided with a sacredotal system which was to last for centuries, as a type of the Priesthood of Christ and his saints; and furnished with a code of laws and sanitary enactments which have been a model for the most civilized peoples of the world.

The very appearance of the camp indicated this marvellous change. In the midst the sacred tent with its brooding cloud, and around it the goodly tents of the people, "as gardens by the river-side, as lign aloes which the Lord had planted, or as cedars beside the waters." The priests and Levites pitched immediately around it, in the inner circle; and around them again the twelve great tribes, three towards each point of the compass, guarding the Tabernacle as a most sacred charge, and as the centre of their national life.

It was a marvellous spectacle, also, when the cloud was taken up, and the priests, through the silver trumpets, gave the signal that the camps on the east side should begin to lead off the march. Then Judah passed on first, followed by Issachar and Zebulun; and the sons of Gershom and Merari, with their six wagons, bearing the heavier portions of the Tabernacle (Num. vii. 1–9) came next;

and after these Reuben, followed by Simeon and Gad; then the long lines of Kohathites, carrying on their shoulders the vessels of the Holy Service; and, lastly, the remaining six tribes in two great divisions, the one led by Ephraim and the other by Dan.

All was beautifully ordered; and though we may not attribute the mighty revolution which had been thus effected to the unaided genius of Moses, we cannot but feel that, as God for the most part gave his teachings, through minds competent to receive and transmit them, so the mental endowments of Moses must have been of no mean order, that he could so readily take, and keep, and transmit the legislation which made Israel a great people. But side by side with this colossal intellect, there was still a weak, human heart, which betrayed itself in the proposal which he made to Hobab.

I. Moses' Proposal.—During their stay at Sinai, it is probable that deputations from neighbouring tribes visited the people, and amongst them was this chieftain of a tribe closely related to Moses by marriage. Hobab, we are told, was the son of Reuel, the Midianite, Moses' father-in-law. Of course, he knew the country well, every foot of it—where the springs lay, and the pastures, and the safest, shortest routes; and so Moses approached him with the request that he would go with them, to give them the benefit of his practical knowledge. "Leave us not, I pray thee; forasmuch as thou knowest how we are to encamp in the wilderness, and thou mayest be to us instead of eyes" (chap. x. 31).

This request was, obviously, most natural. Moses was a very lonely man, as we have seen; and it was pleasant to have one, bound to him by a blood affinity, to unburden himself to, in any special crisis.

At the same time, it was at variance with the general custom, which even then must have commenced strongly to assert itself, of Israelite exclusiveness. This national characteristic was acutely perceived and adverted to by Balaam, when he said: "Lo, the people shall dwell alone, and shall not be reckoned among the nations" (Num. xxiii. 9). The Jew made no intermarriages with neighbouring peoples on pain of death; he dressed in a special garb, and differed from all other men to the very dressing of his beard. And all this, to keep the people free from the plague-spots of the earth, which, in the expressive language of Leviticus (xviii. 25), was "vomiting out her inhabitants."

Even though we admit that at the heart of the nation there were more tender emotions towards any who were willing to sympathize with its spirit—to a Rahab and a Ruth; to the strangers within its gates; and to the Gentiles, who might in after days be attracted by the light which shines from Zion's hill—yet it was an unusual thing for the great lawgiver to go out of his way to utter this winsome invitation to a Midianite prince. And there must have been a strong reason that prompted it.

And shall we not find it in that instinctive shrinking of the human heart from the strange and unknown way? It was because Moses had never gone that way before that he was so eager to obtain Hobab's company, and offered as a bribe that "what goodness the Lord shall do unto us, the same will we do unto thee" (Num. x. 32). How closely home does this phase of thought come to us all! We do not know what may await us at the next turn of the path, or at the top of the pass; what foes may lurk; what emergencies arise; what unexpected barriers arrest our steps. What if we are going into the midst of the foe; or missing a sweet glen with its luscious herbage; or making for a *cul de sac*, through which we shall find no aperture, and must return! And then how shall we survey the place in time to get suitable camping-grounds for the coming hosts! How well to have a Hobab who knows the ground!

We seek our Hobabs in the advice of sage, grey-haired counsellors; in the formation of strong, intelligent, and wealthy committees; in a careful observance of precedent. Anything seems better than a simple reliance on an unseen guide. Now, in one sense, there is no harm in this. We have neither right nor need to cut ourselves adrift from others, who have had special experience in some new ground on which we are venturing. It is a mistake to live a hermit life, thinking out all our own problems, and meeting all our own questions as best we may. Those who do so are apt to become self-opinionated and full of crotchets. God often speaks to us through our fellows; they are his ministers to us for good, and we do well to listen to our Samuels, our Isaiahs, our Johns. But there is also a great danger that we should put man before God; that we should think more of the glasses than of that which they are intended to reveal; and that we should so cling to Hobab, as to become unmindful of the true Guide and Leader of souls. When we have given Him his right place, He will probably restore our judges as at the first, and our counsellors as at the beginning; but the first necessity is that the eye should be single towards Himself, so that the whole body may be full of light.

II. THE FAILURE OF HOBAB, AND THE DIVINE SUBSTITUTE.—The desert chieftain was by no means enamoured of the proposal of his great relative. He had no desire to leave his tribe, his camping-ground, his free, careless existence, to link his fortunes to that great but ill-mannered host.

And other considerations may have weighed with him. It was only a month before that Aaron and his sons had been set apart for their sacred work, and the fire of God had fallen on their dedicatory sacrifices. The people had seen and shouted; but before evening their joy had been shrouded in sudden mourning. For some violation of the sacred ritual, or perhaps, as the subsequent pro-hibition of wine suggests, for personal misconduct whilst engaged in their ministry, the two young priests had been stricken dead, and Aaron forbidden to weep. This must have struck an awful fear through the camp.

Shortly after this, another incident occurred. The son of an Israelitish woman, whose father was an Egyptian, had blasphemed the holy name of God, and cursed in the midst of conflict with a man of Israel. The blasphemer had been stoned. The sentence must have seemed severe, though, as God was King, the sin had amounted to high treason; but the swift and awful vengeance may have been another deterrent cause in influencing the decision of Hobab.

The result of it all was that in reply to Moses' request, he said bluntly, "I will not go; but I will depart unto mine own land, and to my kindred" (ver. 30). Moses still further urged and entreated him; but whether he succeeded or not is doubtful; though there are some reasons for thinking that the second request prevailed, because the descendants of the Kenite are numbered amongst the chosen people (Judg. i. 16).

But it would seem as if his aid were rendered needless by the provision of guidance immediately promised. Up to this moment the position of the Ark had been in the midst of the host, in front of Ephraim, Benjamin, and Manasseh; but henceforth it went three days' journey in front of the people, "to seek out a resting-place for them." We are left to conceive of its lonely journey as it went forward, borne by its attendant band of priests and Levites, and perhaps accompanied by a little group of princes and warriors, and specially by the great lawgiver himself. Far behind, at a distance of miles, followed the camp with its tumult, its murmur of many voices, the cries of little children, the measured tramp of armed bands. But none of these intruded on the silence and solemnity which, like majestic angels, passed forward with that courier group accompanying the Ark, over which cherubic forms were bending. That Moses was there is indubitable; for the august sentences are recorded with which he announced its starting forth and its setting down. In the one case, looking into the thin air, which seemed to him thronged with opposing forces of men and demons, he cried, "Rise up, O Lord, and let thine enemies be scattered, and let them that hate Thee flee before Thee"; and in the other he cried, "Return, O Lord, unto the many thousands of Israel" (verses 35 and 36). Thus God Himself superseded the proposal of Moses by an expedient which more than met their needs.

What consolation there is to each of us, in realizing the spiritual truth underlying this historical fact! We have to pass into the untried and unknown, and know not the way we should take. Some have to go alone. Some with the memory of companions that once went at their side, but whom they will see no more in this life. Some, though at present dowered with dear fellow-pilgrims, are apprehensive and fearful as to the route, and what a day may bring forth. But amid all Jesus is with them, and goes before them, whether for war or rest. He never will forsake nor leave them. And the days as they pass will enable them to say with ever new meaning, "I know whom I have believed."

The Lord Jesus is the true Ark of the Covenant, who has gone before us through the world and death, through the grave and the last rally of the hosts of darkness, to the glory. We have but to follow Him. It is for Him to scatter our enemies, while we stand still and see his salvation. It is for Him to choose our resting-place, while we lie down and prepare ourselves for new obedience.

Let us not anticipate God's guidance or press on Him unduly. "He that believeth shall not make haste." Let there be an interval between the Ark and your steps, so that you may see, so far as possible, what God would have you do; and then deliberately, thoughtfully, but with fixed determination, follow. *He* will "be to us instead of eyes."

And oh, the bliss of knowing that Jesus is not "three days' journey" distant; but near, so that He is ever between us and our foes. Before they can hurt us they must reckon with Him. In Him, too, is rest; so that we may lie under his shadow with great delight, and know that all must be well, since He has chosen our inheritance for us.

XXIII

Noble to the Core

"And Moses said, Enviest thou for my sake? Would God that all
the Lord's people were prophets."
—Num. xi. 29.

UNINTERRUPTED success is hard to bear, much more so than perpetual
trial. This was the moral of the story of the plains of Capua, where
the demoralization, wrought in the troops of Hannibal by the
enervating climate, wrought more havoc than the prowess of the
legions of Rome. Many who were vigorous and energetic when
climbing the steep cliffs of adversity, have succumbed to petty
temptations in days of sunny prosperity.

If it should be debated as to whether sunshine or storm, success
or trial, were the severer test for character, the shrewdest observers
of human nature would probably answer that nothing so clearly
shows the real stuff of which we are made as prosperity; because
this of all tests is the severest. When the younger son came to
possess the portion of goods that fell to him, he went down to feed
swine.

For some two years Moses had been borne along on a flowing
tide. Through faith in the living Jehovah, he had vanquished the
proudest monarch of his time; had conducted nearly three millions
of people through the wilderness wastes without a settled commissariat; had disciplined an unorganized multitude into a mighty
host, with a code of legislation and ritual which is the admiration
of all thoughtful men. This was success enough to turn the head of
any ordinary man; nor could we have wondered if he had shown
signs of undue elation and pride. But the two incidents which we
are now to consider show how absolutely simple and humble he had
remained amid a very summer of success.

ELDAD AND MEDAD.—In condescension to his weakness, his
Almighty Friend appointed seventy colleagues to bear with him

153

the burden of the people; and concerning them the somewhat ominous announcement is made that "the Lord came down in a cloud, and took of the spirit that was upon him and gave it unto them" (Num. xi. 25).

I do not agree with those who think that there was any diminution of the spirit that rested upon Moses. It is very difficult to speak of the sub-division of spirit. You cannot draw it off from one man to others, as you draw off water. The whole Spirit of God is in each man, waiting to fill him to the uttermost of his capacity. It seems to me, therefore, that nothing more is intended than to affirm that the seventy were "clothed upon" with the same kind of spiritual force as that which rested upon Moses.

In each case of those thus anointed, the accession of spiritual force was marked by the sudden breaking forth of prophecy; reminding us of that memorable day, of which this was a miniature, when "they were all filled with the Holy Ghost, and began to speak with other tongues, as the Spirit gave them utterance" (Acts ii. 4). May we not say that the entrance of the Holy Ghost in fulness to the heart of man will always lead to the utterance of thoughts that strive for expression, as the ocean wave sweeps along the sea wall seeking for the inlet where it may expend itself !

For sixty-eight of them the power of utterance was only spasmodic and temporary. "They prophesied, but they did so no more" (R.V.). Emblems are they of those who, beneath some special influence— like that which cast Saul down among the prophets—suddenly break out into speech and act, and give promises not destined to be fulfilled. Two, however, of the selected number, who, for some reason, had remained in the camp, suddenly became conscious of their reception of that same spirit, and they, too, broke out into prophecy, and appear to have continued to do so. Instantly a young man, jealous for the honour of Moses, carried to him the startling tidings, "Eldad and Medad do prophesy in the camp;" and as he heard the announcement, Joshua, equally chivalrous, exclaimed, "My lord Moses, forbid them!" eliciting the magnificent answer, "Art thou jealous for my sake? Would God that all the Lord's people were prophets—that the Lord would put his Spirit upon them !"

It was as if he said, "Do you think that I alone am the channel through which the Divine influences can pour? Do you suppose that the supplies in the being of God are so meagre, that He must stint what He gives through me, when He gives through others ? If it should please Him to create new stars, must He rob the sun of its light to give them brilliance ? Is the gratification of a mean motive of vanity a matter of any moment to me, who have gazed on the face of God ? Besides, what am I, or what is my position, amongst this people, compared with the benefit which would accrue to them, and the glory which would redound to God, if He did for each of them all that He has done for me ?"

This is the spirit of true magnanimity. A spirit of self-aggrandizement is set on retaining its exclusive position as the sole depository of the Divine blessing; though this has the certain effect of forfeiting it, so that fresh supplies cease to pass through. But whenever the eye is single for the glory of God, and position is looked upon only as his gift to be used for his glory, and when the spirit is concentred in one eager and intense desire to see his will done, the glory of that light extinguishes the fires of ambition, and the faithful servant is willing to be anything or nothing, if only the Divine purpose is accomplished.

There is no test more searching than this. Am I as eager for God's kingdom to come through others as through myself ? In my private intercessions can I pray as heartily and earnestly for the success of my competitors as for my own ? Can I see with equanimity other and younger men coming to the front, and showing themselves possessed of gifts which I always considered to be my special province ? Am I conscious of the rising of jealousy or envy when my leadership is subordinated to the claims of rivals ? Should I be willing that the will of God should be done through another, if he suited God's purpose better than myself ? Few of us could answer these questions without the sense of almost insuperable difficulty in assuming the position taken up by Moses when he heard that Eldad and Medad prophesied in the camp.

And yet, in so far as we fall short of that position, do we not betray the earthly ingredients which have mingled, and mingle still, in our holy service ? Yes; it is ourselves that we serve—our schemes, and plans, and selfhood. And if we were to eliminate from Christian service all that has emanated from these sources, what a scanty handful of gold-dust would be left ! Oh, when shall we be able to say, "Would God that all the Lord's people were prophets," and view with thankful joy the levelling up of all Christians to the table-land of our gifts and grace ?

This, however, can never come till we have learnt to spend long hours with God; till we have been taken into his secret place; till we have come to care for his honour more than for our own; till we have become absorbed in the one consuming passion to see Him glorified in his saints, and admired in all them that believe. "The zeal of thine house hath eaten me up." Thus does the herald star, which on the fringe of night has told weary eyes that the dawn is near, sink contentedly into a very ocean of light; though not itself less bright because every inch of space is illuminated with a lustre like its own.

MIRIAM.—We remember her as the little black-eyed, watchful maiden who stood beneath the tall palm-trees of the river's brink to watch the bulrush ark; and again as the heroic woman who answered the deep bass of the delivered host by leading the women's chorus on the shores of the Red Sea. What did she not owe to Moses? But for him she must have been an unknown slave girl, mated to a toiler in Pharaoh's brickfields, the mother of slaves. But now she was free, and the representative woman of an emancipated race, through the brother whom she had rocked in her arms. Ah, it was sad, indeed, that, at the age of ninety, she should turn against him whom she had tended and loved; and that she should poison the mind of the elder brother who had been his spokesman and right hand.

They spoke against him because of the Ethiopian woman whom he had married. Some have thought that Moses had married a second time; but it seems wiser, since the death of Zipporah is not mentioned, to consider the reproach as applicable to her, especially as she probably bore in her complexion the brand of another race. "Cushite" means black, or dark-complexioned. She had comparatively recently come to the camp; and for some time Miriam may have been carefully watching her, with the result, that her whole woman's nature revolted from the thought of having to resign her primacy to such as she was. It is always difficult to see another filling the place which we have looked upon as ours, especially if we are conscious of being able to fulfil its duties better.

How well we can imagine her talking to Aaron and to the women with whom she was intimate, about these "Cushites," until she had raised quite a storm of feeling. This was bad enough in her; but how much worse in Aaron, who held the proudest position in the camp? The function of Moses was temporary, and would pass away with his life; whereas that of Aaron was permanent to himself and his heirs. Yet Aaron could not but feel how vast was the gulf between him and his brother. And out of this there sprang the jealousy which made Zipporah its excuse. "And they said, Hath the Lord indeed spoken only by Moses; hath He not spoken also by us?" How easy it is to disguise jealousy beneath the cloak of zeal for the law of God; and to think ourselves immaculate when rebuking the faults of others.

But how did Moses act—he who, years before, had felled an Egyptian with one blow of his fist? Did he pour out a torrent of indignation, assuring himself that he had just cause to be angry? Did he show them the door of the tent, and bid them mind their own affairs? Did he call on God to strike them down in his anger? Nothing of the sort. He answered not a word; for "the man Moses was very meek, above all the men which were upon the face of the earth" (Num. xii. 3). In his bearing he reminds us of Christ in the judgment-hall, who, "when He was reviled, reviled not again."

Was this weakness, as some would say? Nay, verily ; it was the exhibition of colossal spiritual strength. Only a Samson with unshorn locks could have acted thus. It is the weak man who gives blow for blow; who blurts out his wrath; who cannot control the passion of his spirit. Only the strong man can be perfectly still under provocation, holding himself in, and turning the vehemence of his soul into the heat of an intense love.

It may be well to give some closing rules as to the attainment of this meek and quiet spirit, which in the sight of God is of great price.

First, let us claim the meekness of Christ.—This, of course, was not possible for Moses in the direct way in which it is for us. And yet doubtless, in his case also there was a constant appeal for heavenly grace. The humility of Jesus did not forbid his proposing Himself as our model for meekness. "Learn of Me," He said; "for I am meek and lowly in heart." The likeness of the dove that rested on his head, and the lamb to which he was compared, were the sweet emblems of his heart. And in moments of provocation there is nothing better than to turn to Him and claim his calm, sweet silence, his patience and meekness, saying, "I claim all these, my Lord, for the bitter need of my spirit."

Let us cultivate the habit of silence.—Express a thought, and you give it strength and permanence; repress it, and it will wither and die.

Wisely did the Apostle James lay such stress on the use of the tongue, as the rudder and bit of the whole body; for its use will instantly determine whether the heart is filled with evil or peace. You will often hear it said that the best way of getting rid of an importunate passion is to let it out and have done with it. It is, however, a very mistaken policy. Utterance will give it vigour, and will sow another crop that will soon fruit again. Silence will kill it; as ice kills fish when there are no vent-holes by which they can come up to breathe.

Learn to be still; to keep the door of the lips closed; to give, indeed, an answer when it is asked, and an explanation when it is needed to correct a misapprehension. But for the most part imitate the example of David, who was prepared for his victory over Goliath by the previous victory which he won over his elder brother in the soft answer returned to his insulting questions. "Let every man be swift to hear, slow to speak, slow to wrath" (Jas. i. 19).

Next, consider the harm done by the aggressors to themselves.— The cloud removed from over the tent, as if it must leave the very spot where the culprits stood; and behold, Miriam was leprous, white as snow. There is a piece of profound instruction here; you cannot say unkind or bitter things about another, without hurting yourself more than you hurt him. Like the boomerang of the savage, curses come back to the spot from which they start. And the wronged one may well forget his own anguish as he pours out his soul in pity and prayer for those who, in dealing out their bitter words, have contracted the blot of leprosy on themselves.

Let us leave God to vindicate our cause.—Moses trusted God to vindicate him; and the Almighty God "rode upon a cherub and did fly; yea, He did fly upon the wings of the wind." The Lord heard all that was said, and spake suddenly to the three, and told them that whilst He would speak to others in visions and dreams, it was to Moses only that he would speak face to face, so that he might behold Jehovah's form. "Wherefore then," said He, "were ye not afraid to speak against my servant Moses?" (Num. xii. 8). This is the secret of rest—to cultivate the habit of handing all over to God; as Hezekiah did, when he spread out Sennacherib's letter in the house of the Lord.

Commit yourself to Him that judgeth righteously, in sure certainty that He will vindicate you, and bring out your righteousness as the light, and your judgment as the noonday.

Let us give ourselves to intercessory prayer.—Moses cried unto the Lord, saying, "Heal her now, O God, I beseech Thee" (ver. 13). When we pray for those who have despitefully used and persecuted us, it is marvellous how soon the soul gets calm and tender. We may begin to do it as a duty, in obedience to the command; we soon discover it to be as snow on a fevered forehead, cooling and soothing the soul. Do not wait to feel an inspiration—act on the sense of what your Lord requires; and as you pray, in the calm and holy presence of God, in the secret where your Father is found, you will find that unworthy thoughts will sink, as silt is precipitated to the river-bed, leaving the stream pellucid and clear.

And the Lord heard his servant's prayer, and healed Miriam; but the whole host was delayed a week through her sin. We may be forgiven; but these outbreaks of sin always entail disaster and delay Neither we nor others can be where we might have been had they not occurred.

XXIV

A BITTER DISAPPOINTMENT

"To-morrow turn you, and get you into the wilderness by the way
of the Red Sea."
—NUM. xiv. 25.

IT WAS a weary journey from Kibroth-hataavah to Hazeroth, and
thence to Kadesh, probably the weariest of the entire route. Moses
spoke of it afterwards as "that great and terrible wilderness"
(Deut. i. 19). But at last the hosts reached Kadesh-barnea, on the
very borders of the Land of Promise; within sight of the low hills,
the flying-buttresses, so to speak, of the verdant table-land, which
first arrests the eye of the traveller coming up from the vast limestone
plain of the desert.

How welcome that spectacle, after the four hundred miles of
journey which had occupied the people for the past fifteen months !
Welcome as the land-haze to Columbus, or as his native village
nestling in the embrace of the hills to the returning traveller. It must
have been specially grateful to the eye of Moses.

I. HIS HOPES.—As yet God had graciously veiled from him the
weary journeys of the forty years that were to succeed. He had no
idea of them. They had never entered into his calculations. From
the way in which he spoke to the people, he evidently counted on a
comparatively brief struggle, sharp, but short, through which they
would pass to their possession. It never occurred to him that any
one but himself would plan that campaign, even if Joshua led it;
or that any other hand would settle the people in the land of their
eager longings. These are the words he addressed to the people as
they camped in sight of the rolling prairies of Canaan: "Ye are come
unto the mountain of the Amorites, which the Lord our God doth
give unto us. Behold the Lord thy God hath set the land before

thee; go up and possess it, as the Lord God of thy fathers hath said unto thee; fear not, neither be discouraged" (Deut. i. 20, 21).

As he said these words, must there not have been, deep in his heart, a sigh of relief now his task was almost done, and he might lay down his weighty responsibilities? God's glory was secured beyond their power to tarnish its lustre. The Egyptians and all the neighbouring nations must hear and be convinced. And as for himself, surely there were in store some few happy years in which he should repose after the long toils of his life. "Ah, sweet Land, of which God has spoken to me, surely there is within thy precincts some sequestered nook, where I may sit down and rest, and review an accomplished work!"

Who can doubt that some such hopes and thoughts as these filled his soul, and whispered the one deep sweet word, Rest—Rest? No more the daily gathering of manna; because it was a land of wheat and barley, in which they should eat bread without scarceness. No more the quenching of thirst at the water that flowed hot over the desert sand; because there would be vines, and fig-trees, and pomegranates: it was a land of brooks of water, of fountains and depths that sprang out of valleys and hills. No more the pitching and striking of tent, the setting of the watch, the perpetual movement; for every man would sit under his own vine and fig-tree. After a few years spent thus, he might ask to depart in peace, and pass home from the Canaan of earth to the Sabbath-keeping of heaven.

Is it not thus that we all picture to ourselves some blessed landscape, lying warm and sunny under the smile of heaven? Life is pretty hard just now: a march over a great and terrible wilderness; a stern fight; a bearing of burdens, for which we have only just got strength enough. But never mind, it cannot last—there must be respite; the long lane must have a turning; the wilderness-march must have a Canaan; the lack of sympathy and tenderness must be swallowed up and forgotten in the embrace of a love which shall obliterate the memory of all, so that we shall awake as out of a brief, unpleasant dream. But suppose it be not so! What if He who loves us better than we love ourselves has marked our stations in a desert-march, that lead right up to the mount from which we are to ascend to our Father's home! What if we are to fight with Moab, and meet Balaam, and see every one of those with whom we commenced life droop around us! What if we are to lie down to die alone beneath his kiss, away from the prattle of children, and the warm pressure of loving hands, on some Pisgah height! All this may be so; but if it is so, how will we do? Yet this is precisely what came to Moses.

II. THE QUARTER FROM WHICH HIS DISAPPOINTMENT CAME.—
It came entirely from the people. *Their first mistake was in desiring to spy out the land.* It is certainly said in these chapters that "the Lord spake unto Moses, saying, Send thou men, that they may search the land of Canaan" (Num. xiii. 1, 2). But the proposal did not emanate from the Lord. It had another origin, which was disclosed by Moses himself forty years afterwards, in words that followed those quoted above, "And ye came near unto me, every one of you, and said, We will send men before us, and they shall search us out the land, and bring us word again" (Deut. i. 22).

As in the case of Saul, the King of Israel, God gave them what they would have. Their self-will was a profound mistake. Had not God promised to give them the land, and could they not trust his choice? Were not his eyes ever upon it, from the beginning to the end of the year? Why need they wish to spy it out? What about his promise to give it them; why, then, need they be so anxious to see whether they could cope with its possessors? They had but, as Moses said, to go up and possess that which He had given.

Their second mistake was in receiving the discouraging report of the majority of the spies. Up to a certain point there was perfect agreement between them. "We came into the land whither thou sentest us, and surely it floweth with milk and honey, and this is the fruit of it." Then the ten said, "The people are strong, the cities are fenced and very great; and, moreover, we saw the children of Anak there. . . . We be not able to go up against the people, for they are stronger than we" (verses 28, 31, R.V.). But the two, Caleb and Joshua, whose names alone linger on our tongues as household words, replied, "If the Lord delight in us, then He will bring us into this land, and give it us" (Num. xiv. 8).

The difference between the two lay in this, that the ten looked at God through the difficulties, as when you look at the sun through a reversed telescope, and it seems indefinitely distant and shorn of its glory; while the two looked at difficulties through God. And the people sided with the ten, and turned aside from the thought of God, to dwell long and sadly on the stupendous obstacles that menaced their occupation of the land. Here was a fatal mistake.

Unbelief never gets beyond the difficulties—the cities, the walls, the giants. It is always picturing them, dwelling on them, pitting them against its own resources. Faith, on the other hand, though it never minimises the difficulties, looks them steadily in the face, turns from them, and looks up into the face of God, and counts on Him. This is what the people failed to do; and for this they lost Canaan. "And the Lord said unto Moses, How long will this people not believe in Me" (chap. xiv. 11, R.V.). "We see that they could not enter in, because of unbelief" (Heb. iii. 19).

Note, that they lost Canaan, not because of the graves of lust, but because of their unbelief. My brother, do not sit down beside that grave of lust, and suppose that that is going to settle your future. Never ! God is not going to tether you for ever to a grave. There is a resurrection and a new life before you, even for you; arise in the light of his forgiveness, and walk through the length and breadth of the land to possess it. Know thou this, that the only thing which can exclude thee thence is that thou wilt not believe in a forgiveness and grace, which are like the blue arch of heaven above thee, or like the immensity of eternity itself.

Their next mistake was in their murmuring, which proposed to substitute a captain for their tried friend and God-given leader. "All the congregation lifted up their voice and cried; and the people wept that night. And all the children of Israel murmured against Moses and against Aaron, and said, Would God tna   had died in the land of Egypt. . . . And they said one to another, Let us make a captain, and let us return into Egypt" (chap. xiv. 1–3).

This was perhaps the bitterest hour in Moses' life. They had proposed to elect a captain before, but it was when he was away; this proposal was made before his face. The people whom he had loved with passionate devotion, whose very existence was due to his intercession on the Mount when they were on the point of being destroyed, had forgotten all he had done; actually proposed to supersede his authority; and if he would not go with them beneath their new-made captain, to leave him to his own devices there. And he fell on his face before all the assembly of the congregation. What unutterable agony rent his breast !—not only that he should be thus set aside, but that the anger of God should be thus provoked by the people he loved !

And as he lay there, did he not also, in those dark, sad moments, see the crumbling of his fairy vision, the falling of a shadow over the fair prospect of his hopes; as when a pelting shower of rain hides a landscape which a moment before had lain radiant in the summer light ? So it has befallen in our own experience, not once, nor twice. We had been on the point of realizing some long-cherished hope. We were within a day's march of it. Our hands had already reached across the frontier line, and plucked the first fruits and pressed the luscious grapes of Eshcol to our lips. Oh, rapture ! oh, fruition of long expectation ! oh, heaven of bliss ! Then suddenly there is some one or more to whom we are tied, and their education is not complete. They cannot yet go over into the good land ; and because they cannot, we may not. And as we stand there, the voice says, "To-morrow turn you, and get you into the wilderness by the way of the Red Sea" (chap. xiv. 25).

III. His Refusal to Escape the Disappointment.—The dream of Moses for a speedy entrance into the land might even yet have been realized. If all the people were cut off, and he spared to be a second Abraham, the founder of the nation, it might be possible even yet for him to pass into the good land, and like Abraham settle there. And thus the trial came into his life. Satan tempts us, to reveal the evil in us ; God to reveal the good. So God, knowing the hidden nobleness of his faithful servant, and eager that it should be revealed to all the world, suggested to him a proposal, that He should smite the people with pestilence, and disinherit them, and make of him a nation greater and mightier than they.

"Accept it," said the spirit of the self-life, "thou hast had trouble enough with them; it will only hasten the inevitable issue of their misconduct; besides, think of the rest thou wilt enter and the renown which will accrue to thee in all after-time." "No," said his nobler, truer self. "It may not be; what would become of Jehovah's fame ? and how can I endure to see my people cut off?"

There are few grander passages in the whole Bible than that in which Moses puts away the testing suggestion as impossible. "If Thou shalt kill all this people as one man, then the nations which have heard the fame of Thee will speak, saying : Because the Lord was not able to bring this people into the land which He sware unto them, therefore He hath slain them in the wilderness" (verses 15, 16). Then quoting the words which God had spoken into his heart on that memorable occasion when He passed down the mountain gorge, he pleaded that He would pardon the people according unto the

greatness of his mercy, as He had been doing from the first of leaving
Egypt until then. In other words, Moses would not have the rest he
longed for at the sacrifice of a ray of God's glory, or of the people
with whom his life was linked, though they had sadly plagued and
disowned him. And so he turned away from the open gate into
Paradise, and again chose rather to suffer with the people in their
afflictions than enjoy the pleasures of Canaan alone. Let us ponder
the lesson; and when next a dear delight is within our reach,
and it will be more for the glory of God and the good of others to
turn from it, let us ask grace to take the rugged path of the wilderness, though it mean a lonely life for forty years, and a death on
Pisgah.

IV. A CONTRAST TO HIS ENDURANCE OF DISAPPOINTMENT.—
Little is said about the leader's bearing. He kept silence, and opened
not his mouth; he hid his face even from good, because God did it.
But the people's behaviour throws his into strong relief.

When they heard that they were to wander in the wilderness for
forty years, till their carcases fell in its wastes, to be interred in the
sands as winding-sheets, they rose up early in the morning, and gat
them up to the top of the mountain, saying "Lo, we be here, and
will go up unto the place which the Lord hath promised . . . Nevertheless the ark of the covenant of the Lord, and Moses, departed
not out of the camp" (verses 40, 44). By force of will and energy
they sought to reverse the sentence just passed on them. Moses
meekly bowed his head to it, and accepted the discipline of those
long years.

Do not times like this come into our lives? We have come to
the brink of some great opportunity, and the prize has seemed
within our reach. But by some outburst we have shown ourselves
unable or unfit to possess it. God puts us back. He says in effect,
You are not yet fit to enjoy the blessing. You must go back to the
common round, sit at the daily task, plod around the dull mill-
wheel. Exercise yourself in toils and frets and trifles, which are not
worthy of a place in history; and after awhile come back and stand
before these gates again, and you shall be admitted.

But we will not submit to it. "Nay, but we will go up." We will
storm the position ; we will not be thwarted. It is a hapless and useless
resolve. You cannot force the gate. Better a hundred times wait
meekly outside, learning the lesson of patience and faith, and you

shall stand there again ere long to find it open to the summons of your ennobled and purified spirit.

V. MOSES' SOLACE IN DISAPPOINTMENT.—Yet there were springs at which that weary spirit slaked its thirst. The sense that he did the will of God; the blessedness which unselfishness always brings to the elect spirit; the joy of seeing the result of the Divine discipline in the growing earnestness and strength of his people; the reception of daily grace for daily need. All these were his.

But even better than these there was the growing realization that the true rest of which he dreamed was not to be found in any earthly Canaan, however enticing; but in that rest of heart, that Sabbath-keeping of the soul, that repose of the nature in God, which is alone permanent and satisfying, amid the change and transience of all human and earthly conditions. So our God not unseldom breaks up our earthly visions, dear and cherished, in order that our soul, bereaved and solitary, may search for and find those diviner things which the moth of change cannot gnaw into, and the rust of time cannot corrode. "These things God worketh oftentimes with man."

XXV

Faithful under Reproach

"O God, shall one man sin, and wilt Thou be wroth with all the congregation?"

—Num. xvi. 22.

Few men have had greater experience of the ingratitude of their fellows than Moses. Here it broke out again, and this time in a formidable conspiracy led by Korah, with whom were associated two hundred and fifty princes, men of renown. The special points were the position he held and the authority he exercised; and the revolt throws some interesting light on the manner in which God's servants should consider the position they occupy in his church.

In the history of all workers for God there will come crises, when wrong motives will be imputed and unkind suggestions passed from mouth to mouth, even by those whose spiritual life has been due to their prayers and tears. Now it is jealousy of growing influence; then it is unwillingness to accept directions and fall in rank at the word of command; again it is the dislike of a carnal soul at the high spiritual demands which are in direct collision with its longings for milk and honey, fields and vineyards. Such disaffection begins with one discontented sensual soul; but it spreads as fire in prairie grass. There are many craven hearts ready enough to follow, who would not dare to lead, in an attempt to subvert some eminent and devoted servant of God. Sometimes the pretext is no better than in the case of the man who voted for the expulsion of Aristides, for no other reason than that he was tired of hearing him called "the Just."

At such times we do well to turn to this dark chapter in the history of the forty years' wanderings, and learn how men ought to behave themselves in the house of God, which is the church of the living God, the pillar and ground of the truth.

I. Look on Your Position as God's Appointment.—Korah and his confederates suggested that Moses and Aaron had taken on

167

themselves the offices which they held, the one as king in Jeshurun, whenever the heads of the people gathered; the other, with his family, as priest. "Why should these offices be exclusively vested in the two brothers ? Were there not plenty of men as good as they ? Was not all the congregation holy ? And might not the presence of Jehovah be had by others as well as by them ?" It was a conspiracy of princes against the leader and prince, and of Levites against the priestly family.

Instantly Moses fell on his face before God—his favourite attitude for meeting these outbreaks of popular hatred and discontent—like the bulrush which meekly bows its head as the autumn blast sweeps over the moor. But he made no further attempt to justify his position or Aaron's. He might have alleged his past services, his claims on the gratitude and loyalty of the people; he might have reminded them that their national existence was due, under God, to his faith, his prayers and tears, his intercessions and exertions on their behalf. But on all these points he held his peace, and took the whole matter into the Divine presence, throwing the responsibility on his God.

First, *he reminded the malcontents that their own position had been assigned by the appointment of the Most High.* The God of Israel had separated them from the congregation of Israel, to bring them near unto Himself, to do the service of the tabernacle of the Lord, and to stand before the congregation to minister unto them. It was distinctly *He* who had brought them near, and all the sons of Levi with them. There was, therefore, no cause for jealousy. The places of influence and authority in Israel were not a lottery, where some men might happen to draw prizes and others blanks. Posts were assigned to men, and men to posts, by the distinct interposition of God. And they who had been so distinctly appointed surely should admit that an equally distinct Divine appointment had been made in respect of Aaron and himself.

Next, and as a result of such a conception of the true position of affairs, *this ebullition of anger was shown to be really directed against God Himself.* "Therefore thou and all thy company are gathered together against the Lord; and Aaron, what is he that ye murmur against him?" (ver. 11, R.V.) When men turn against us, we are too apt to run away from our position in panic; to make terms with them; or to throw down the reins in a pet. Any of these courses is a profound mistake, and quite incompatible with a right apprehension of our position towards God on the one hand, and man on the other.

There are many passages which show beyond doubt that our positions in the visible church are defined as carefully as of members in the human body. Though you be only a joint or hinge, on which other members articulate and work, you must believe that your position was fixed by the All-wise and Almighty Disposer of all. Is it to be supposed for a moment that He, who appointed the place where each star should shine in the bosom of night, should leave the position of the stars of his church to chance? (Acts xx. 28; 1 Cor. xii. 28; Eph. iv, 11, R.V.).

If, then, disaffection or dissatisfaction arise, they must not in themselves determine your course. It may be that they indicate that the time has come for you to go elsewhere. But this evidence is by no means conclusive. You must go to Him who sent you, whose servant you are, and ask if it is his will for you to vacate your post; and if so, that He should make it clear. If He does not, then let nothing that man can do alarm or trouble you. You must stand to your post, as the lonely sentinel amid the falling lava of the eruption, till the Commander of the Lord's hosts tells you that you may surrender your sacred charge. But if no such orders come, grace and patience will; and you must remain till relieved by death.

Lastly, *Moses left the ultimate decision with God.*—They were all to take censers, which were the ordinary pre-requisites of the priests alone; and having charged them with fire and incense, were to present themselves before the Lord, at the door of the tent of meeting. It would be then for God to choose who should be holy, and who should be caused to come near unto Him.

What infinite rest would come into the lives of many of God's servants, if only they drank in the spirit of this heroic soul!—so resolute to do the Divine will, at all hazards; and to remain at the helm, though the fire of popular resentment crept along the bulwarks and blistered the skin from his hands. How often the face is worn with care, and the head streaked with grey, even if the course of the life be not deflected from the straight rule it should follow by thoughts like these—What will my committee, or elders, or supporters say? What will become of my children's bread, if I thwart so influential a contributor? How shall I be able to withstand so strong a popular movement? Must I not yield to the suggestions of friends, or threatenings of foes? Alas! these questions are so often asked, and the course of life decided by the weighing of prudential suggestions, and the consideration of human policy, but with little or no reference to Him, whose slaves we are, selected and appointed for special work.

Let us act as Moses, the faithful servant did, and refer all to the decision of our Master and Lord; and in the meanwhile be at peace. It is such a profound mistake to carry the burdens of the Lord's work. When difficulties come, as they will, they are his quite as much as they are ours. We have no right to carry his anxieties and care for his cares. He asks us to do his work; to obey his behests; to fulfil his commissions; and to transfer all the weary pressure and burden to Himself. If the people do not like us, it is for Him to determine whether He will continue us in our position; and if He choose to do so, He must keep us there, and give us favour with them. If our supplies fall off in doing his work, He must maintain us and our dear ones. A royal court is bound to support its own embassies. If our mission involve the assumption of leadership which is disputed by our fellows, we cannot recede from it, so long as we can say with Moses, "The Lord hath sent me to do all these works, for I have not done them of mine own mind" (ver. 28). Thus pride and jealousy are alike impossible. We know we receive nothing except it is given us from heaven; and we refer all disputants to Him who has put us where we are.

II. CHERISH KINDLY FEELINGS TOWARDS THOSE WHO OPPOSE.— How nobly Moses dealt with this murmuring crowd ! When first he heard their contentious voices, he assumed the posture of intercession, and began to plead for those who despitefully used and persecuted him. When it seemed, on the following morning, as if God would destroy not the ringleaders only, but all the congregation who assembled with them at the door of the tent of meeting, he fell on his face and pleaded with the God of the spirits of all flesh not to punish all for the sin of one man. Dathan and Abiram, the sons of Eliab, were specially contumelious; and, when he sent to summon them, returned an insulting message, accusing him of betraying them with false representations, asking why he had not led them into the land of milk and honey. They went so far as to insinuate that they dared not come, lest he should bore out their eyes (ver. 14). Moses was naturally very indignant and wounded by these bitter and undeserved reproaches; but he made no attempt to answer them, except in self-vindication before the Lord. And when bidden he did not hesitate to rise up, and go to them, with no trace of vindictiveness in his address.

And on the following day, when the people, unawed by the terrible judgments that had befallen, murmured against Aaron and himself, and accused them of having killed the people of the Lord, he again averted from them the judgment which was threatened—first by his prayers, and then by hastening Aaron to stand, censer in hand, between the plague-stricken and those as yet unreached by the sickle of death. How quick he was to know when wrath had gone out from the Lord ! How eager to stay its progress ! How generous to make such efforts on the behalf of those who had but an hour before launched at him their bitter reproaches!

This is the true pastor's heart. He partakes of the spirit of the Good Shepherd, who loved those who taunted Him, and pleaded for the forgiveness of his murderers. There is no more resentment in his heart towards those who oppose Him than in a mother's towards the babe who, in its paroxysm of temper, smites her breast with its tiny hands. The grey-headed retainers, who, prepared to die, resist the entrance of the mob at the palace gates, that by their blood they may purchase time for their royal master's escape, do not take the malice of the bloodthirsty crowd as a mere personal matter, since they know that they are hated as his representatives, and are proud to suffer for him. Oh for that chivalrous devotion to Christ, that we may only suffer in fellowship with his sufferings, die only in conformity to his death, identified with Him in all ! It is, perhaps, the loftiest summit of devotion when we crave love only to pass it on to Him; and dread hatred only because it hurts the hearts that cherish it, and inflicts a wrong on the dear and glorious Lord.

III. You May Expect God to Vindicate You.—"And Moses said, If these men die the common death of all men . . . then the Lord hath not sent me. But if the Lord create a creation (*marg.*), and the ground open her mouth and swallow them up . . . then ye shall understand that these men have despised the Lord. And it came to pass, as he made an end of speaking all these words, that the ground clave asunder that was under them, and the earth opened her mouth and swallowed them up" (verses 28–32, R.V.). It was a terrible act of vengeance. It was essential to the existence of the camp that the mutiny should be stamped out without mercy. There was no help for it. The cancer must be cut out of the quivering flesh. The death would be painless for the little ones, and though cut off from life here they would pass at once into the broad and blessed spaces of eternity; but for the rest the punishment was merited, and their extermination saved the camp.

Many have essayed to stamp out the church of God; but, like Haman, have been hanged on the gallows prepared for Mordecai. Others have spoken against the servants of the Lord, but have suffered untimely and terrible deaths. The bears out of the wood have devoured. Herod has been eaten by worms. Persecutors have died in horrible torment. No weapon that has been formed against God's saints has prospered. Every tongue that has been raised against them in judgment has been condemned.

Trust Him, O suffering saints, doing his will in the teeth of opposition and hate! Fear not the faces of men; be not dismayed before their threats—He is with you to deliver you. They may fight against you, but they shall not prevail; their proudest threats shall fail of their fulfilment, as the sea-billow which flings itself on the boulder is dissolved into a cloud of harmless spray. God loves his saints. They are all in his hand. But especially those are in its covert who are engaged in his sacred work. If only they are faithful to Him and to his behests, and live on his plan, there is nothing He will not do for them. When they call upon Him in their distress, He will deliver them from their strong enemy, and bring them into a large place; because He delights in them, and they put their trust in Him.

XXVI

How it went Ill with Him

"And Moses lifted up his hand, and with his rod he smote the rock twice."
—Num. xx. 11.

It was but one act, one little act; but it blighted the fair flower of a noble life, and shut the one soul, whose faith had sustained the responsibilities of the Exodus with unflinching fortitude, from the reward which seemed so nearly within its grasp.

The wanderings of the forty years were almost over. The congregation which had been scattered over the peninsula had converged towards the given meeting-place in Kadesh. There the encampment remained for some months; and there Miriam died—one of the few with whom that lonely spirit could still hold converse of that life which lay beyond the desert sands, the valleys of Sinai, and the waters of the Red Sea, in the distant mighty land of the Pharaohs and the Pyramids. Aaron, Caleb, Joshua (and perhaps the Levites), were the only relics and survivors of that vast triumphant host, whose voices had rung out their challenge on the morning of emancipation; and each of the four thought himself sure, and his comrades also, of going over to "see the good land that is beyond Jordan, that goodly mountain, and Lebanon." But this was not to be.

I. How it Befell.—The demand of the people on the water supply at Kadesh was so great, that the streams were drained; whereupon there broke out again that spirit of murmuring and complaint which had cursed the former generation, and was now reproduced in their children. Oblivious to the unwavering care of all the preceding years, the people assembled themselves together against Moses, and against Aaron, though it was against Moses that they principally directed their reproach.

They professed to wish that they had died in the plague that Aaron's censer had stayed. They accused the brothers of malicious designs to effect the destruction of the whole assembly by thirst. Although the cloud of God brooded overhead, and the manna fell day by day, they cursed their abiding-place as evil. They taunted Moses with the absence of figs, vines, and pomegranates. They demanded water. And this was the new generation of which he had cherished such high hopes, the new growth on the old stock ! It could hardly have been otherwise than that he should feel strongly provoked.

However, he resumed his old position, prostrating himself at the door of the tent of meeting until the growing light that welled forth from the secret place indicated that the Divine answer was near. Unlike the injunction on a similar occasion, which now lay back in the haze of years, Moses was bidden, though he took the rod, not to use it; but to speak to the rock with a certainty that the accents of his voice, smiting on its flinty face, would have as much effect as ever the rod had had previously, and would be followed by a rush of crystal water. Yes, when God is with you, words are equivalent to rods; the gentlest whisper spoken in his name will unlock the secrets of rocky chambers, and roll away great stones, and splinter sepulchres where entombed life awaits a summons. Rods are well enough to use at the commencement of faith's nurture, and when its strength is small; but they may be laid aside without hesitance in the later stages of the education of the soul. For as faith grows, the mere machinery and apparatus it employs becomes ever less; and its miracles are wrought with the slightest possible introduction of the material. Years ago you were bidden to use the rod because your faith was untried; but by this time the greater faith should work through a slighter and more fragile means.

Moses might have entered into these thoughts of God in quieter and more tranquil moments; but just now he was irritated, indignant, and hot with disappointment and anger. When, therefore, the assembly was gathered together in their thronging multitudes around him, he accosted them as rebels. He spoke as if the gift of water depended on himself and Aaron. He betrayed his sense of the irksomeness of their demand, and then vehemently smote the rock with his rod twice. And as those blows re-echoed through the still air, they shivered for ever the fabric woven by his dreams and hopes.

The vision that had allured him through those long years faded as light off Alpine snows at sunset; and angels were sent to choose the site beneath the cliffs of Pisgah, where his body should keep guard at the gate of the Land, in which he had hoped to lie. What a warning is here, admonishing us that we sometimes fail in our strongest point; and that a noble career may be blasted by one small but significant and for ever lamentable failure! "The Lord said unto Moses and Aaron, Because ye believed not in Me, to sanctify Me in the eyes of the children of Israel, therefore ye shall not bring this assembly into the land which I have given them" (ver. 12, R.V.).

The people did not suffer through their leader's sin. The waters gushed from out the rock as plentifully as they would have done if the Divine injunctions had been precisely complied with. "The water came forth abundantly; and the congregation drank, and their cattle." Man's unbelief does not make the power of God of none effect: though we believe not, yet He remaineth faithful; He cannot deny Himself, or desert the people of his choice.

II. THE PRINCIPLE THAT UNDERLAY THE DIVINE DECISION. (1) *There was distinct Disobedience.* No doubt was possible as to the Divine command; and it had been distinctly infringed. He was not to strike, but to speak; and he had twice smitten the rock. In this way he had failed to sanctify God in the eyes of the people. He who ought to have set the example of implicit obedience to every jot and tittle, had inserted his own will and way as a substitute for God's. This could not be tolerated in one who was set to lead and teach the people.

God is sanctified whenever we put an inviolable fence around Himself and his words; treating them as unquestionable and decisive; obeying them with instant and utter loyalty; daring to place them high above all dispute as the supreme rule and guide of conduct. Therefore, when Moses set them aside to follow the behest of his own whim, it was equivalent to a desecration of the holy name of God. "Ye did not sanctify Me in the eyes of the children of Israel."

It is a solemn question for us all whether we are sufficiently accurate in our obedience. It is a repeated burden of those sad chapters of Hebrews, which tell the story of the wilderness wanderings —the cemetery chapters of the New Testament—that "they could not enter in because of unbelief." But throughout the verses the margin suggests the alternative reading of *disobedience*; because disobedience and unbelief are the two sides of the same coin—a coin of the devil's mintage. They who disobey do not believe; and they who do not believe disobey. May the great High Priest, with his sharp, two-edged sword, pierce to our innermost heart, to cut away the least symptom of disobedience; then shall faith be strong, and through its gates we shall pass into the land of rest.

(2) *There was Unbelief.*—It was as if he had felt that a word was not enough. As if there must be something more of human might and instrumentality. There was a too evident reliance upon his own share in the transaction, or on the mysterious power of the rod which had so often wrought great wonders. He thought too much of these, to the exclusion or dwarfing of God's eternal power. He did not realize how small an act on his part was sufficient to open the sluice-gates of Omnipotence. A touch is enough to set Omnipotence in action.

It is very wonderful to hear God say to Moses, "Ye believed not in Me." Was not this the man by whose faith the plagues of Egypt had fallen on that unhappy land; and the Red Sea had cleft its waters; and the daily manna had spread the desert floor with food; and the people had marched for thirty-eight years unhurt by hostile arm ? What had happened? Had the wanderings impaired that mighty soul, and robbed it of its olden strength, and shorn the locks of its might, and left it like any other ? Surely, something of this sort must have happened! One act could only have wrought such havoc by being the symptom of unsuspected wrong beneath. Oaks do not fall beneath a single storm, unless they have become rotten at their heart.

Let us watch and pray, lest there be in any of us an evil heart of unbelief; lest we depart in our most secret thought from simple faith in the living God; lest beneath a fair exterior we yield our jewel of faith to the solicitation of some unholy passion. Let us especially set a watch at our strongest point. Just because we are so confident of being strong there, we are liable to leave it unguarded and un-watched, and therefore open to the foe. So shall we be saved from a fall that shall shut the gates of Canaan against us, and consign us to an unknown and untimely grave.

But how much there is of this reliance on the rod in all Christian endeavour ! Some special method has been owned of God in times past, in the conversion of the unsaved, or in the edification of God's people, and we instantly regard it as a kind of fetish. We try to meet new conditions by bringing out the rod and using it as of yore. It is a profound mistake. God never repeats Himself. He suits novel instrumentalities to new emergencies. He puts new wine into new bottles. Where a rod was needful once, He sees that a word is better now. It is for us to consult Him, and to abide by his decision; doing precisely as He tells us, and when, and where.

(3) *There was the spoiling of the type.*—"That Rock was Christ"; from whose heart, smitten in death on Calvary, the river of water of life has flowed to make glad the city of God, and to transform deserts into Edens. But death came to Him, and can come to Him but once. "Christ was once offered to bear the sins of many." "The death that He died, He died unto sin once; but the life that He liveth, He liveth unto God." "I am He that was dead; and behold, I am alive for evermore." These texts prove how important it was to keep clear and defined the fact of the death of Christ being a finished act, once for all. It is evident that for the completeness of the likeness between substance and shadow, the rock should have been stricken but once. Instead of that, it was smitten at the beginning and at the close of the desert march. But this was a misrepresentation of an eternal fact; and the perpetrator of the heedless act of iconoclasm must suffer the extreme penalty, even as Uzzah died for trying to steady the swaying ark.

But there was something even deeper than these things. There was an eternal fitness in the nature of the case in Moses not being permitted to lead the people into the land of rest. Moses represented the law. It came by him; and he therefore fitly stands before the gaze of the ages as the embodiment of that supreme law, whose eye does not wax dim or its force abate, under the wear and tear of time. But the law can never lead us into rest. It can conduct us to the very margin and threshold, but no further. Another must take us in, the true Joshua—Jesus, the Saviour and Lover of men.

III. THE IRREVOCABLENESS OF THE DIVINE DECISIONS.—Moses drank very deeply of the bitter cup of disappointment. And it seems to have been his constant prayer that God would reverse or mitigate his sentence. "Let me go over, I pray Thee, and see the good land that is beyond Jordan, that goodly mountain, and Lebanon (Deut. iii. 25). No poet could have painted that land with more glowing colours. He dipped his brush in rainbow tints as he spoke of that good land—that land of brooks and fountains and depths; that land of wheat and barley, of vines and pomegranates and figs; that land of oil, olives, and honey. And no patriot ever yearned for fatherland as Moses to tread that blessed soil. With all the earnestness that he had used to plead for the people, he now pleaded for himself. But it was not to be. "The Lord was wroth, and said unto me, Let it suffice thee; speak no more unto Me of this matter." The sin was forgiven; but its consequences were allowed to work out to their sorrowful issue. There are experiences with us all in which God forgives our sin, but takes vengeance on our inventions. We reap as we have sown. We suffer where we have sinned.

At such times our prayer is not literally answered. By the voice of his Spirit, by a spiritual instinct, we become conscious that it is useless to pray further. Though we pray, not thrice, but three hundred times, the thorn is not taken away. But there is a sense in which the prayer is answered. Our suffering is a lesson warning men in all after-time. We are permitted from Pisgah's height to scan the fair land we long for, and are then removed to a better. We have the answer given to us in the after-time, as Moses, who had his prayer gloriously fulfilled when he stood with Christ on the Transfiguration Mount. And in the meanwhile we hear his voice saying, My grace is sufficient for thee; my strength is made perfect in weakness.

But oh that God would undertake the keeping of our souls!—else, when we least expect it, we may be overtaken by some sudden temptation; which befalling us in the middle, or towards the close of our career, may blight our hopes, tarnish our fair name, bring dishonour to Him, and rob our life of the worthy capstone of its edifice.

XXVII

PREPARING FOR PISGAH

"And Moses said unto them, I am a hundred and twenty years old this day; I can no more go out and come in: also the Lord hath said unto me, Thou shalt not go over this Jordan."

—DEUT. xxxi. 2.

JUST before the dark River through which Pilgrims pass to the City of Gold, Bunyan places the land of Beulah; where the sun ever shines, the birds sing, and every day the flowers appear on the earth. The air is very sweet and pleasant. It is within sight of the City, but it is beyond the reach of Giant Despair; and they who come thither cannot so much as see the turrets of Doubting Castle. And in some such blissful experience saintly men have sought to spend a brief parenthesis between the press of life's business and their entrance into the welcome of Christ. But such was not the experience of Moses. The last year of his life was as full of work as any that had ever passed over his head.

There was, first, the conquest of Eastern Canaan.—Dean Stanley speaks of it as that mysterious eastern frontier of the Holy Land, so beautiful, so romantic, so little known. Its original inhabitants had been expelled by the kindred tribes of Moab and Ammon; but they, in their turn, had been dispossessed of a considerable portion of the territory thus acquired, by the two Canaanite chiefs, Sihon and Og, whose names occur so frequently in this narrative.

The attack of the Israelites was justified by the churlish refusal of Sihon to the request that they might march through his borders on their way to Jericho. He not only refused them passage, but gathered all his people together, and went out against Israel on the frontier line between his territory and the wilderness. The song which commemorated the victory lays special emphasis on the prowess of the slingers and archers of Israel, afterwards so renowned: "We have shot at them; Heshbon is perished." These words suggest the probable reason for the overthrow of this powerful monarch, under the providence of God. The sword followed on arrow or stone, so that the army was practically annihilated; no further resistance was offered to the march of the victorious foe. The cities opened their gates; and this fertile region between the Arnon and the Jabbok, consisting of "a wide table-land, tossed about in wild confusion of undulating downs, clothed with rich grass, and in spring waving with great sheets of wheat and barley," came into possession of the chosen people.

But this was not all. North of this lay Bashan, which has been described by Canon Tristan and others as a rich and well-wooded country, abounding in noble forests of oak and of olive trees, interspersed with patches of corn in the open glades. It was and is the most picturesque and the most productive portion of the Holy Land. Og, its king, was renowned for his gigantic stature. According to Josephus' narrative, he was coming to the assistance of Sihon, when he heard of his defeat and death. But, undaunted, he set his army in array against the hosts of Israel. The battle took place at Edrei, which stood to guard the entrance of a remarkable mountain fastness; and it ended in the complete victory of Israel. The result is told in the strong, concise narrative of Moses. "They smote him, his sons, and all his people, until there was none left him remaining; and they possessed his land."

Nothing could have accounted for the marvellous victories, which gave Israel possession of these valuable tracts of country—with cities fenced with high walls, gates, and bars, together with a great many unwalled towns—but the interposition of God. He had said beforehand, "Fear not! I have delivered him into thy hand;" and so it befell. Immense swarms of hornets, which are common in Palestine, seemed to have visited the country at this juncture; so that the people were driven from their fortresses into the open plains, where they were less able to stand the assault of the Israelites.

Moses, at their urgent request, proceeded to allot this rich and beautiful territory to the Reubenites and Gadites and the half-tribe of Manasseh, after receiving their solemn pledge to bear their share in the conquest of Western Palestine. "I commanded you," he said afterwards, "that ye shall pass armed before your brethren, the children of Israel, until the Lord give rest unto your brethren, as unto you."

Next came his last charge to the people. This was delivered in a series of farewell addresses, which are contained in chapters i–xxx of the Book of Deuteronomy. This book is to the four preceding ones much what the Gospel according to John is to the other three. It is full of the most pathetic and stirring appeals. Memory of the past, gratitude, fear, self-interest, are the chords made ·to vibrate to this master-touch. Well may it be said of Moses that he loved the people; and in these pages we may trace the course of the molten lava which poured from his heart.

The key-phrases of that remarkable book are: Keep diligently; Observe to do; and, The Lord shall choose. It abounds with exquisite descriptions of the Land of Promise, which may be spiritually applied to those rapturous experiences denoted by the phrase, The Rest of Faith. It is, indeed, as old Canaan was, a good land, a land of brooks of water, of fountains and depths springing out of the valleys and hills. There we drink of the river of the water of life; there we eat the bread of life without scarceness, and lack nothing that we really need. The 28th chapter anticipates the Beatitudes of our Lord's Sermon on the Mount; and happy is he that can appropriate them in blissful experience, and go in to possess the land.

In our judgment the much-debated question of authorship is settled by the distinct affirmation of the New Testament. Take, for instance, the quotation of Deut. xxx. 11–14 in Rom. x. 6–10. The Apostle Paul distinctly speaks of Moses as having written these words.

Next came his anxiety about a successor.—Moses spake unto the Lord, saying, "Let the Lord, the God of spirits of all flesh, set a man over the congregation, which may go out before them, and which may go in before them; which may lead them out, and bring them in, that the congregation of the Lord be not as sheep which have no shepherd." In answer to this request, he had been directed to take Joshua, the son of Nun, in whom was the Spirit, to bring him before Eleazar, the priest, and before all the congregation, and to give him a charge. This he seems to have done; but as death drew near he apparently gave him a second charge (compare Num. xxvii. 16, 17, and Deut. xxxi. 7, 8).

What a striking scene it must have been when, on his one-hundred-and-twentieth birthday, the aged law-giver called unto Joshua, and said unto him in the sight of all Israel, "Be strong and of a good courage: for thou must go with this people unto the land which the Lord hath sworn unto their fathers to give them; and thou shalt cause them to inherit it. And the Lord, He it is that doth go before thee; He will be with thee; He will not fail thee, neither forsake thee; fear not, neither be dismayed." Immediately afterwards the pillar of cloud stood over the door of the Tabernacle, and Moses and Joshua were summoned to present themselves before God in its sacred precincts. There, in almost identical words to those which He had spoken by the lips of Moses, God gave Joshua his commission to bring the children of Israel into the land which He had sworn unto them, together with the promise that He would be with them.

His last acts were to arrange for the custody of the Law and the perpetuation of its reading.—He did the first by depositing the book, in which he had recorded the Divine revelations made to him, in the side of the Ark of the Covenant. It was to be kept under the custody of the Levites; and passages were to be read from it at the end of every seven years, when all Israel appeared before God in the place which He should choose.

And as to the second, Moses put his exhortations and entreaties into two magnificent odes, the one dealing out warnings against apostasy, the other dwelling seriatim on the characteristics of the tribes, and giving them a parting blessing, after the fashion of the dying Jacob.

The thirty-second chapter of Deuteronomy is one of the sublimest human compositions on record. It was Moses' swan song. It is the store from which later Scripture writers draw plentifully. It has been called the Magna Charta of Prophecy. It is worthy to be compared to one only song else, the Song of the Lamb, with which it is combined by the harpers on the margin of the glassy sea: "They sing the song of Moses, the servant of God, and the song of the Lamb."

The repeated comparisons of God to a Rock; the lavish kindness with which He had treated his people since He first found them in a desert land; the comparison of the Eternal to a mother eagle in teaching its young to climb the unaccustomed steeps of air; the ingratitude with which his marvellous kindness had been requited; the dread fate to which their rebellion must expose them; the mercy with which their repentance would be greeted—all these are recorded in glowing, eloquent words, that stand for ever as a witness of how stammering lips may speak when they have been touched with the live altar coal. Or take the closing verses of the Benediction on the tribes. The lonely glory of the God of Jeshurun, who rides on the heavens to help and save his people; the home which men may find in his eternal nature; the underpinning everlasting arms; the irresistible might with which He thrusts out the enemy from before the forward march of the soul He loves; the safe though isolated dwelling of Israel; the fertility of the soil and the generosity of the clouds; the blessedness of having Jehovah as the shield of help and the sword of excellency—all these features of the blessed life are delineated by the master-hand of one who dipped his brush in the colours mixed by his own experience.

What glimpses we get of the inner life of this noble man ! All that he wrought on earth was the outcome of the secret abiding of his soul in God. God was his home, his help, his stay. He was nothing: God was all. And all that he accomplished on the earth was due to that Mighty One indwelling, fulfilling, and working out through him, as his organ and instrument, his own consummate plans.

Thus Moses drew his life-work to a close. Behind him, a long and glorious life, before, the ministry and worship of the heavenly sanctuary. Here, the shekinah; there, the unveiled face. Here, the tent and pilgrim march; there, the everlasting rest. Here, the promised land, beheld from afar, but not entered; there, the goodly land beyond Jordan entered and possessed. What though it was a wrench to pass away, with the crowning-stone not placed on the structure of his life; to depart and be with God was far better !

XXVIII

THE DEATH OF MOSES

"So Moses, the servant of the Lord, died there in the land of Moab,
according to the word of the Lord. And He buried him i n a valley in the
land of Moab, over against Beth-peor."
—DEUT. xxxiv. 5, 6.

THE BIBLE is the book of *life*. Its pages teem with biography; they
contain but scant memorials of death. The only death they describe
at length is that of Him who in dying slew death. The very minuteness
of the description there shows how unique and all-important it was.
Men make more of death than of life as a gauge of character. A
few pious sentences spoken then will go far to efface the memory
of years of inconsistency. God makes most of life.

The records of Scripture find little room for dying testimonies,
words, or experiences; whilst they abound in stories of the exploits
and words of those who have stormed and suffered and wrought in
life's arena. This may explain why, contrary to human custom and
expectation, the death of the great Lawgiver is described with such
brief simplicity.

But this simplicity is only equalled by the sublimity of the conception. After such a life it was meet that Moses should have a death
and burial unparalleled in the story of mankind ; and we do not
wonder that poet, painter, and preacher, have found in that lonely
death on Pisgah's summit a theme worthy of their noblest powers.
We can but cull a few wild flowers as they caress that mountain
brow; more we must leave to others. Moses' death casts a light
on sin, and death, and dispensational truth.

I. ITS BEARING ON SIN.—We cannot suppose that the sudden
outburst of impetuous temper at Meribah—when his spirit was
agitated by a fierce whirlwind of wrath, as a storm sweeping down

184

some mountain rent on an inland lake—could remain long unforgiven. As far as the east is from the west, so far had that transgression been removed. But though the remission was complete, yet the result lingered in his life, and shut him out from an experience which should have been the crown of his career.

"The Lord hath put away thy sin," said Nathan to the royal transgressor; but "thy child shall die, and the sword shall not depart out of thy house." The dying chief was pardoned; but he suffered in his body the extreme penalty of his sin. The mistrust which hinders a man from accepting all the benefits of Christ's Ascension is put away; but nothing can compensate him for his loss. Never a word may be spoken about the evil courses that have wrecked the health and fortunes of the Prodigal; but though he sits at his father's board, he can never be in health or vigour or overflowing joy, as he might have been if he had never wandered forth.

Nor does sin only entail loss and sorrow on the transgressor; it robs mankind of much of the benefit which otherwise had accrued from his life. If it had not been for his want of faith and his passionate behaviour, Moses had led his people across the Jordan, and served them for many an after year.

Let not the ease of pardon ever tempt thee to think lightly of sin, or to imagine that it leaves no traces on soul or life, because it is secure, through penitence and faith, of God's forgiving mercy. If one act of mistrustful anger laid Moses, the friend and servant of God, in a desert grave on the frontiers of the Land, what may it not do for thee?

II. Its Bearing on Death.—*Its Loneliness*. That majestic spirit had ever lifted itself, like some unscaled peak, amid other men. Into its secrets no foot had intruded, no human eye had peered. Alone it wrought and suffered, and met God, and legislated for the people. But its loneliness was never more apparent than when, unattended even by Joshua, he passed up to die amid the solitudes of Nebo. Alone he trod the craggy steep; alone he gazed on the fair landscape; alone he laid down to die.

But in that loneliness there is a foreshadowing of the loneliness through which each of us must pass unless caught up to meet the Lord in the air. In that solemn hour human voices will fade away, beloved forms retire, familiar scenes dim to the sight. Silent and onely, the spirit migrates to learn for itself the great secret. Happy the man who, anticipating the moment, can say: "Alone, yet not alone, my Saviour is with me. He who went this way by Himself is now re-treading at my side."

Its Method. We die, as Moses did, "by the word of the Lord." It is said in the Hebrew legend that one angel after another sought to take his life in vain. First, there came the one who had been his special instructor; but his courage failed him when he essayed to destroy the fabric on which he had spent so much pains. Then the angel of death was summoned to undertake the task. He eagerly approached him; but when he saw the wondrous lustre of his face shining like the sun, and heard him recite the prodigies of his career, he, too, shrank back abashed.

And when these great angels had given up the work as surpassing their loftiest powers, Moses turned to the Almighty (so the legend runs) and said, "Thou, Lord of the Universe, who wast revealed unto me in the burning bush, remember that thou didst carry me up into thy heaven, where I abode forty days and forty nights; have mercy upon me, and hand me not over into the power of the angel of death."

This, of course, is the picturesque form in which the love and reverence of after generations elaborated these wonderful words, which tell us that Moses died "by the word of the Lord." Some still further substituted "kiss" for "word"; so that it seemed as if the Almighty had kissed away the soul of his faithful servant, drawing it back to himself in a long, sweet, tender embrace.

Is not this the manner in which all saints die? Their deaths are precious to the Lord, and after the troubled day of life—agitated in its early morning by the trumpet calling to battle; fretted through an overcast noon by the pressure of its responsibilities and cares; lit in the evening by the rays of a stormy sunset, piercing through the cloud-drift, the tired spirit sinks down upon the couch, which the hands of God had spread, and He bends over it to give it its good-night kiss, as in earliest days the mother had done to the wearied child. That embrace, however, is the threshold, not of a long night of insensibility, but of an awakening in the supernal light of the everlasting morning.

Its Sepulchre. We are told that "the Lord buried him in a valley in the land of Moab," in spite of the opposition of the Evil One, who contended with the archangel sent to secure that noble deserted shrine. What had the archfiend to do with it? Did he desire to make it vie with the temple of the living God, filching honours which the people would be only too glad to give? We know not; but his purpose was ignominiously frustrated. God cared for the dead body of his child. Not even the king of terrors could make it distasteful to the Father's love. Though in ruins, the temple was precious. And so even a band of angels was not permitted to perform the sacred work of interment. We are told that *He* buried him; as if the Almighty would not delegate the sacred office to any inferior hand. And is it not attributable to the love of God that through the love of friendly hearts the last rites are rendered to the bodies which Christ has purchased?

As we trust God to supply the needs of the body in life, so let us trust Him for its burial in death. He marks where the dust of each of his children mingles with its mother earth. When a grave is opened, his eye rests on it; and though no foot may ever tread its soil, no hand keep it decked with flowers, He never forgets it; and none will be overlooked when the archangel blows his trumpet over land and sea.

Its Purpose. We are told that "the children of Israel wept for Moses thirty days;" and if we connect this statement with the fact of the unknown grave, we shall be able to discern the Divine purpose in its concealment. We often underrate the living, and have to wait until they are removed from us to estimate them truly.

Few men have had greater claims on their fellows than Moses. He had sacrificed his high position in Pharaoh's court to bear his people as a nurse through the ailments of their childhood. He had enjoyed unparalleled opportunities of fellowship with God. He had wielded uncommon power: at the bidding of his faith winds had brought meat; rocks had gushed with water-springs; the sea had parted and met; the desert-floor had been strewn with food. Is it not more than likely that, if the Lord had not concealed his grave, the valley of Bethpeor would have become a second Mecca, trodden by the feet of pilgrims from all the world? It was best to make such idolatry impossible. The hidden grave forced the people to turn from earth to heaven.

Is not this God's policy with us? When Lazarus is dead, the sisters send for Jesus. When the groud is blasted, the pilgrim in the weary land turns to the shadow of the great Rock. When no place is found for the sole of her foot, the dove makes for the window of the ark. When the supply fails from the rock-cisterns, we are driven to the stream which flows from the throne of God. This is why your home is desolate, and your heart bereaved. It is for this that he who was to you what Moses was to the people has been removed.

> *For e'en the cloud*
> *That spreads above, and veiled love,*
> *Itself is love.*

Its Vision. From the spot on which he stood, without any extra-ordinary gift of vision, his eye could range over an almost unequalled panorama. At his feet, the far-away tents of Israel; to the north, the rich pasture-lands of Gilead and Bashan, bounded by the desert haze on the one hand, and on the other by the Jordan valley, from the blue waters of the Lake of Galilee to the dark gorge of the Dead Sea. And beyond the river he could sweep over the fair Land of Promise, from the snow-capped summits of Hermon and Lebanon to the uplands of Ephraim and Manasseh; with the infinite variety of cities perched on their pinnacles of rock, of cornfields and pasture lands, of oil, olives, figs, vines, and pomegranates. Immediately before him, looking West, was Jericho, in its green setting of palm-trees, connected by the steep defile with Jerusalem; not far from which Bethlehem, on the ridge of the hills, gleamed as a jewel.

So to dying men still comes the vision of the goodly land beyond the Jordan. It is not far away—only just across the river. On fair days of vision, when some strong wind parts the vails of mist and smoke that too often dominate our spiritual atmosphere, it is clearly visible. But the vision is most often reserved for those who are wait-ing on the confines of the Land, ready for the signal to enter. They tell us that on that border-land they hear voices, and discern visions of beauty and splendour, of which heart had not conceived. Dr. Payson said, shortly before he died, "The Celestial City is full in my view. Its glories have been upon me; its breezes fan me; its odours are wafted to me; its sounds strike upon my ears; and its spirit is breathed into my heart." May God grant us the blessedness of dying on the hill-top with that vision in our gaze.

III. THE BEARING ON DISPENSATIONAL TRUTH. The Law came by Moses; and Moses stands on the plains of history as the embodiment, as he was also the vehicle, of the moral law, whether given from Sinai or written on the fleshy tablets of the human heart.

It was in perfect keeping with this conception that there was no decay in his natural vigour. His eye was as a falcon's, his step lithe and elastic, his bearing erect. He did not die of disease, or amid the decrepitude of old age; "he was not, because God took him." Time had only made him venerable, but not weak. And thus he represents God's holy law, which cannot grow outworn or weak, but always abides in its pristine and perfect strength, though it cannot bring us into God's rest.

Of that rest it is not possible to speak here. Canaan does not primarily represent the rest which awaits us on the other side of death, where the fret and chafe of life are over; but the rest which may be entered here and now, in which the soul is set free from the tyranny of self and corruption, and abides in the peace of God which passes all understanding. Then life becomes one blessed succession of trustful obedience to the will of God; then, too, we are satisfied with the abundant wealth stored up for us in God, and He makes us drink of the river of his pleasure. This is the goodly Land of promise, which can only be seen from afar by those who know nothing except what Moses can teach them; but may be entered by those who follow the Ark through the river of death to the self-life and forward to resurrection ground.